CUBE
Bead
Stitching

CUBE
Bead
Stitching

Contemporary jewelry designs you can make

Virginia Jensen

KALMBACH BOOKS

Kalmbach Books
21027 Crossroads Circle
Waukesha, Wisconsin 53186
www.Kalmbach.com/Books

Published in 2009
13 12 11 10 09   1 2 3 4 5

Manufactured in the United States of America

ISBN: 978-0-87116-281-6

Publisher's Cataloging-in-Publication Data

Jensen, Virginia, 1941-
   Cube bead stitching : contemporary jewelry designs you can make / Virginia Jensen.

   p. : ill. (some col.) ;   cm.

   ISBN: 978-0-87116-281-6

1. Jewelry—Design. 2. Jewelry making—Handbooks, manuals, etc. 3. Beadwork—Patterns.
4. Beadwork—Handbooks, manuals, etc. 5. Decoration and ornament—Handbooks, manuals, etc. I. Title.

TT212 .J46 2009
739.27

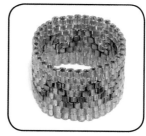

Contents

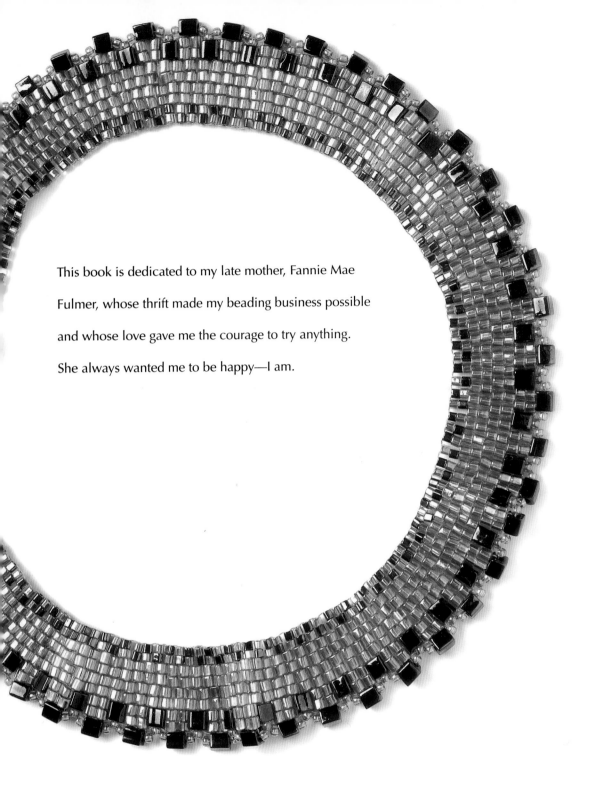

This book is dedicated to my late mother, Fannie Mae

Fulmer, whose thrift made my beading business possible

and whose love gave me the courage to try anything.

She always wanted me to be happy—I am.

The purpose of this book is threefold. First, I want to share my love for cube beads and the fun I've had working with them. I hope they flourish in the marketplace and offer all of us even more color choices and finishes to rival the availability of regular seed beads and Japanese cylinder beads.

Secondly, I had a few flashes of inspiration shortly after I started working with these beads, and they resulted in what I think are some unusual designs and new variations on old stitches I'm eager to share. I think most beaders will enjoy making these projects. I can't think of a better way to spread joy.

And finally, I've learned most of what I know about beading from books. I'm grateful to all of the authors who took the time and energy to write down the instructions and take the step-by-step photos from which I learned the skills I now have. This is my thank you. Passing on knowledge and accomplishments is part of a healthy, thriving craft. It stirs up the creative juices and pushes us all to new heights of accomplishment.

Why cube beads?

When cube beads hit the U.S. market in the early 2000s, only two sizes were available: 3 and 4 mm. I loved the contemporary look they gave my bracelets and appreciated the nuances of texture they produced. When smaller, 1.5 mm cubes appeared on the scene, I immediately ordered some and started creating a similar effect on a refined scale.

My first explorations were working with cube beads on a small loom and in herringbone and peyote stitches. With loomwork and peyote, the cubes locked up tightly if I wasn't careful. Herringbone produced flexible, beautifully textured pieces. But the most fun came when I started to play with the mechanics of St. Petersburg chain—cubes just love St. Pete. Many of the interesting variations that resulted are within the pages of the book you hold.

Pieces stitched with cubes have a unique surface that reflects light in a different way than a piece made of traditional seed beads. People often notice that my cube bead work has an unusual quality, although the reason isn't obvious until I point out that the beads are square, not round. Cube beads have held my interest from the time I first picked one up, and I still haven't begun to exhaust their potential. I hope you'll find them fascinating too.

Introduction

Working with Cube Beads

About Cube Beads

Japanese bead manufacturers Toho and Miyuki are the primary exporters of cube beads to the United States. Your bead store or supplier may carry one brand or the other, or a mix. Although you will see slight differences between the brands, it's more often the size and the color that will affect your decision as you choose cube beads for the projects you make.

Toho cubes have square holes, positioned so that each corner points to a flat side of the bead. This creates a very secure lock when you draw two beads together with thread. The corners of Toho cubes tend to be rounded. Toho cube beads are available in 1.5, 2, 3, and 4 mm.

Miyuki beads have sharper corners than Toho cubes and holes that are round. The Miyuki sizing is slightly different: 1.8, 3, and 3.5 mm. For our purposes, because we're talking about differences that are mere tenths of a millimeter, the Miyuki 1.8 mm can be interchanged with the Toho 1.5 mm, and the 3.5 mm can be interchanged with the 4 mm.

The projects in this book primarily use Toho cubes, with Miyuki cubes as possible substitutions. There is one exception, and that is the Russian Waltz necklace, which uses small, hollow sterling silver cubes.

In some projects, you may notice I call for size pairings where the larger bead is twice the size of the smaller bead—this creates pleasing patterns of size relationships.

You may encounter a few other types of cube beads, but most of them are too large and have holes that are too small for these projects.

Flexibility

Generally, we want our beadwork to be flexible; we appreciate the drape and cling of a bracelet or necklace. But at other times, rigidity can be an asset. One of the areas I've explored in this book is a type of construction that puts the cubes in a series of interlocked boxes, holding them in the shape of a star, a tree, or a heart, for example. I've also explored ways to help the cubes drape, as in my collar that drapes beautifully around the neck, and ways to make a loop of cube beads bend smoothly.

Cube or square?

Truly square cube beads are rare; finding one would be like finding a four-leaf clover. I would be pleased to see the regularity of Japanese cylinder beads in cube beads. These cubes begin as a long glass rod with four flat sides. The rod is cut into tiny cubes, and the cuts don't always break evenly, so you'll need to cull any oddball shapes.

I tell my students that the manufacturers and retailers are responsible for what they put on their shelves, but you are responsible for what you put in your beadwork. Keep a discriminating eye on the quality of bead you are picking up with your needle. This is a good practice for every beader, beginner or advanced.

Toho vs. Miyuki comparison (top row to bottom): 4 mm Toho, 3.5 mm Miyuki, 3 mm (left two are Miyuki and right two are Toho), 2 mm Toho.

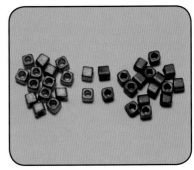

The smallest cubes: Miyuki's 1.8 mm (left) and Toho's 1.5 mm.

The equipment I use most often: my needle and thread, a few bowls of beads, scissors, and my clip-on magnifiers, which I seem to need more often these days.

My favorite scissors.

For me, shallow white sauce bowls work best for picking up beads.

Tools and Materials

This is primarily a book of designs. Other beading books, magazines, and resources can provide a studied and comprehensive list of supplies and techniques. With that in mind, I do not attempt to be exhaustive here, but rather I will share with you what works for me.

If you're experienced or motivated, you may prefer skimming the information below and jumping right into a project. No matter what your experience level, I encourage you to read, explore, and experiment with products new to the market to determine what works best for you.

What you need for the projects

Grab the sharp little scissors and the needle threader from your sewing kit, and a few shallow sauce bowls from the kitchen. Pick up your beads, findings, a pack of beading needles, and thread. For those of you eager to get started, that's the short list. If you would like more detail, read on.

My primary tools are my needles and my scissors. I use James or Pony brand needles in sizes 10 and 12. The #10s are my favorites because they are sturdy enough that I don't bend them out of shape, and they fit well in the cubes' larger holes. I keep a needle threader handy for when the thread gets soft from wear. I have two pairs of scissors: one is a sharp, slender embroidery scissors that I use for getting in close to snip off tails, and the other is a small pair of sharp craft scissors for cutting my thread.

For laying out and picking up beads, I use small, shallow sauce bowls. I like them better than ceramic palettes because palette segments are too small. Try to find the bowls in white, without any pattern to confuse the eye. I run the needle into the bead and slide it up the curved edge. By the time I'm at the top, the needle is pointed up and the bead won't fall back into the bowl. I can move my bowls of beads around according to what I'm focusing on.

I use a pair of bentnose pliers to hold jump rings as I'm attaching thread. I use them along with chainnose pliers when I'm attaching clasps.

Occasionally, I use a pair of magnifying glasses that clip onto my regular glasses. When I need them, they're indispensable. You may prefer a magnifying hood, drop-down magnifier lenses, or magnifying lights. I use these mostly when I'm tying off, undoing a tangle of thread, or sewing on a clasp—wherever I need extra care.

All the projects in this book are made using only needle and thread except one. That exception is the Russian Waltz necklace, which incorporates the simple wirework technique of making loops in wire or head pins. (Even that project has an option in which you use only needle and thread if you prefer.) For the wirework, you will need two pairs of pliers and a pair of fine wire cutters. Making simple loops takes a little practice, but a good set of instructions or a good instructor can help a lot if you're having trouble. It's a good skill to learn.

Beading thread

You can buy thread for beading that is made from linen, silk, cotton, nylon, and a new generation of high-tech, super-strong synthetics. I once found thread made from bamboo! Each of these materials has its pros and cons.

Most people learn beading on a nylon thread such as Nymo or C-Lon. These and similar threads have been developed or adapted for beading and are available in most beading stores and from catalogs. Every so often a new brand of nylon thread will come on the market, and it's hard to keep up with them all. Their biggest advantage is that they come in a wide variety of colors and often in more than one weight. I keep a selection of Nymo or C-Lon on hand for times when I want to match colors closely.

Fireline is a fishing line, and it's strong enough for any beading project. It comes in clear, neon green, and dark gray. I like the dark gray color for working with black or very dark beads. Fireline is springy, and it tends to kink, much like fine wire, so it will not hang well if the beadwork hasn't enough weight to pull it straight.

For strength, flexibility, solidity, and lack of stretch and abradability, I prefer gel-spun, braided polymer fishing line—Power Pro by brand name.

If you haven't worked with fishing line lately, this is not the stiff, yellowish monofilament your grandfather used. The new thread is made using strands of an ultra-high molecular weight polyethylene, an organic polymer molecule of carbon and hydrogen. This is the material used in bullet-proof vests. It's hard to break or fray and doesn't decay in sunlight. The multiple filaments are braided in a special machine to prevent twisting and looping. (This is so fishermen don't get tangled up in their line, but it's an advantage to us beaders, too.)

When I'm designing, I often redo a section of beading two or three times to get something just right. With polymer line, I don't have to discard every experiment because of frayed thread. I work a lot with repeating patterns, and if I make a mistake, I simply take it out and rework the pattern correctly. I don't have to cut the thread and tie on new when I can just undo the error and move on. Also, when you're working with cube beads, your thread is more likely to rub against a hard and sometimes sharp edge, especially with uncoated and matte-finish cubes. Power Pro works great in all these situations.

Here are a few comments on why this thread has become such a favorite of mine and a few tips on working with it:

Stretch: If you've ever made a necklace and found later that the thread has started to show, the beads are sagging, and all your fine work needs to be redone, you'll appreciate the lack of stretch in this polymer

line. It helps me keep good tension in my beadwork, and this is crucial in designs where the shape has to be maintained. Many pieces in this book are like that. The construction of interlocking boxes in St. Petersburg chain relies on the cubes not slipping out of place.

Treating thread: I usually don't. Cube beads have big holes, and the resin coating on Power Pro usually works well to reduce friction. If I'm having a bad tangling day (who knows what causes these—humidity, bad thoughts, solar flares?), I'll use Thread Heaven to help the tails keep their distance from each other. But even that cannot always change a bad thread day. It's just a fact of beading life.

Splitting: Many beading threads have parallel filaments that are easily divided with the sharp tip of the needle, leading to precious minutes of untangling if you split the thread or have to back out of a bead situation. Because it's braided, the polymer line tends to hold together and roll away from the needle tip.

Knotting: Knotting is easy because this line is so flexible. I tie a lot of surgeon's knots, and occasionally I have to untie one. When I do, the braiding helps me get hold of the thread with my needle; doing this with a parallel-fiber thread is a nightmare.

Gluing: I like to secure my knots with glue. My favorite cyanoacrylate glue, Loctite Super Glue Gel Control, has the most user-friendly dispenser that I've found. It lasts a long time without drying out, it dispenses in the tiniest drops, and the tip doesn't clog. Because the polymer line is so inert, the glue doesn't make it brittle with time as it does other beading threads.

Cutting: Some people have difficulty cutting the braided polymer fishing line. I cut it with the same small pair of craft scissors I use for cutting fine beading wire, and they work great. After several years of cutting this line, they are still doing their job. Another option is a pair of small, sharp wire cutters that you reserve for cutting the polymer line. Some Power Pro packaging includes a cutter that works well too.

Color: All the gel-spun polymer threads have a color coating that may come off as a fine powder as you work. Before you start work, you can pinch a clean tissue between your fingers and run the length of thread through a few times until the coating no longer comes off.

You will have to choose from among colors that are made for fishing, but that isn't so bad. White is a standard, but I only use this when working with very light colors and with transparent or translucent beads to keep from muddying the bead color. Moss green is the color I use most as it blends with most medium-range cool hues. You can also get red and yellow, plus a light blue—often available only in winter because it's for ice fishing! Many bead stores and suppliers now carry the polymer lines for beading, or you can try your local sporting goods store. For all the weights in all the colors, try one of the big fishing suppliers on the Internet.

Weight: Gel-spun polymer thread comes in a variety of weights from 5- to 250-lb. test strength. I use either 8- or 10-lb. test because it works well in my favorite #10 beading needle. You can use 5- to 8-lb. test and a #12 needle for finer work. For simple bead stringing, the 20-lb. test works great.

Durability: My favorite thread story illustrates this thread's durability. I made a watch band using 10-lb. test Power Pro and wore the watch daily for many months. I began to wonder how long the thread would last. One day a bead broke. I replaced it and continued to wear the watch. Months later, I noticed the clasp had broken. I replaced the clasp, congratulating myself on choosing such good thread. Months passed again and, after a day of serious furniture moving, I found I had cracked the watch crystal. Unfortunately, I have not been able to find a replacement watch to fit the band. But the band—and the thread—are still intact, waiting for another lifetime.

Findings

These projects call for two broad categories of findings—earring findings and clasps. When making earrings, you can choose lever-back findings (my favorite), hook-style earring wires, or post-style findings. In clasps, choices include lobster claws, S-hooks, toggles, magnetic, box, and slide-locks, among others.

I like toggle clasps for simple bracelets. I find them easiest to fasten and the most secure. The toggle should slip easily into the loop, and the sides of the toggle should be longer than the inner diameter of the loop so the toggle won't work its way out during wear. I avoid magnetic clasps, though some I know swear by them. I use a lot of S-clasps with jump rings on either end for single-strand necklaces.

If your bracelet or necklace is wider than about three quarters of an inch, aesthetics call for a wider clasp. A box clasp is a good choice. I like the slide-lock clasp even better for bracelets. For a wider necklace such as the Checkered Collar or the Chain of Chevrons, you might consider a more decorative clasp with a two- or three-ring attachment and a chain.

Jump rings and knots

In many of these projects, you will fold your thread and attach the loop to a jump ring. These rings must have the opening soldered closed to keep the fine thread from slipping out of the space between the ends. I use a lot of these. I keep a couple of sizes of both sterling silver and gold-filled jump rings in my findings box.

I like soldered jump rings for attaching earrings in particular. There is usually a front to the earring, and I want it facing out and slightly forward. To do this, I attach the starting thread to a jump ring with a lark's head knot. It holds the thread in a stable position, better than just running it through the ring or tying it onto the ring. Depending on how the work starts, I might spread the two threads even farther apart by adding additional half-hitches on either side of the knot; this helps when you are starting with larger beads or with two strands of work.

I often use a jump ring to attach the earring to the earring wire as well. The metal-on-metal attachment is fluid, and the earring swings gracefully without turning too far to either side.

I also use jump rings on segments of beadwork that have to attach to another element, as in the Russian Waltz necklace. I find them better for starting a single-strand necklace than the usual clamshell bead tips; I've had clamshells pull apart because the thin strip of metal that attaches to the clasp is pretty weak. It's a good idea to have some bigger jump rings to use with clasps. Often, a clasp will come with a jump ring that is not soldered closed or no jump ring at all.

You can find soldered jump rings at beading stores and findings suppliers. Notice whether the measurement is inner diameter (ID) or outer diameter (OD). When I call for a small jump ring, use a 22-gauge, 3 mm OD ring. If your vendor goes by inner diameter, order 2 mm. Gauge tells you how thick the wire is; a smaller number is a thicker wire and vice versa. For a clasp, choose a larger, thicker jump ring, such as 5 mm or 6 mm, 18- or 20-gauge.

Attaching thread to a soldered jump ring

Here is an easy way to attach a jump ring to a folded length of thread: Put the loop of thread upward through the ring, reach through the loop with a pair of pliers, and grasp the ring [a]. With your fingers, pull the loop down and around the ring, and it will lock into a lark's head knot [b].

a

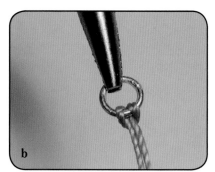
b

My Beading Survival Pack

There is no end of wonderful stuff you can buy, but I'll offer a minimalist guide here. If I had to take my beadwork to a desert island (a pretty happy thought, actually), this is what I would take, in order of importance:

- **#10 needles and a threader**
- **My sharp scissors**
- **Power Pro and Fireline**
- **3 or 4 shallow sauce bowls**
- **Cyanoacrylate glue**
- **Jump rings in gold and silver**
- **Chainnose and bentnose pliers**
- **Magnifying glasses**
- **All the beads and findings I could pack**

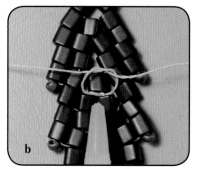

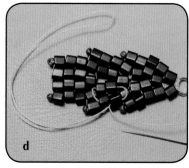

Finishing Tips

To finish their thread, some beaders run the tail back in several directions through the work without knotting. This may work well enough for small-holed 1.5 mm cubes if the piece is large enough to secure a few inches of tail. When you are making a small piece like an earring, however, you probably will not have room to do this.

Cube beads have larger holes than many types of round seed beads, and, of course, the larger the cube bead, the larger the hole. Finishing off simply by running thread back and forth just doesn't work when you're using beads with larger holes; be sure to do some kind of knotting in addition.

No matter what type of piece I'm working on, I almost always tie some type of real knot to finish off (in fact, I'm rather obsessive about this). Tying a **half-hitch knot [a]** in two or three spots as you run the thread out through the work may be sufficient.

Many of the pieces in this book are made with a symmetrical technique leaving two tails, one on each side of the piece. I like to bring the two tails together at the center near the hole of a bead and tie them in a **surgeon's knot [b]**. A surgeon's knot is a square knot with one of the wraps doubled.

I like to tie the doubled wrap first and pull it into place, then tie the single wrap in the opposite direction. I pull it almost closed so there is a small loop of crossed thread right over the first tie, then I dot my glue in the center of the double wrap. When I pull the single wrap tight, it closes onto the dot of glue. The glue is in the center of the knot, not all over my work. Then I pull the knot into the nearest bead, hiding it completely, run the tails out through a few beads **[c]**, and trim.

Here's a trick to use if you don't have two tails. You will need at least 10 in. (25 cm) of thread to do it.

Take your working thread back through the bead your thread is exiting, leaving a loop about 3 in. (7.6 cm) long. Go through a few adjacent beads in a circle so the thread is exiting the same bead as the loop **[d]**. Tie the loop and the single thread together in a surgeon's knot, and pull the knot into a bead. Thread a needle onto the loop, run each tail through the work, and trim. (If you have trouble threading the loop onto a needle, cut the loop open and thread each tail separately.)

I've noticed that if a tail is going to show itself in a finished piece of work, it is usually at the end, where it may spring out from the last bead or two. I tie a half-hitch a couple of beads from the end. It helps if you make the last bead you go through the largest one you can get to. This decreases the chance of it popping out.

TIP One problem many beginning beaders have is that they don't leave long-enough tails. You need a minimum of 6 in. (15 cm) and at least 12 in. (30 cm) if you're going to attach a clasp. Thread is cheap. Be generous with your tails.

About the Projects

Skill level

The skill level of the projects in this book ranges from beginner to intermediate. If you have never done any of these stitches, you could begin with some of the simpler designs and work your way up to the more complex pieces. Within the categories—bracelets, necklaces, and so on—each section goes from easiest to most challenging. When I introduce a new stitch, that project includes a review of the basics of that stitch, and every project includes complete instructions.

Copyright and responsibilities

When I was first learning beading from published designs, I was not clear about my rights and responsibilities; I wished someone would spell it out for me. Now I would like to do that for you.

What you *may* do: You may make any and all of these projects for yourself and in a limited number as gifts for friends or family. What you *may not* do: You may not earn money from these projects by making and selling them, by claiming a design as your own, by teaching them, or by copying the projects and distributing them.

I know that people like to get together and work on projects. And I know people often need the help of a local teacher to figure out some of the more complex designs. Teachers, simply ask each of your students to buy a copy of the book, and then you can all work on the projects together.

Copying designs

People want to know what constitutes copying designs, and there is a subtle distinction here. If I make a simple herringbone bracelet with 3 mm cubes and gold beads in a certain pattern, that doesn't mean no one can ever make another herringbone bracelet. It isn't the herringbone bracelet or the cube beads that carries the rights, but that certain pattern. Go ahead and make a herringbone bracelet with 3 mm cube beads, but create a new pattern. Then you have your own design, to which you own the rights. This distinction is an important one. It's how design grows and flourishes as we build on one another's work. Simply put, what belongs to the designer isn't the use of the beads or the use of the stitch, neither of which can be copyrighted, but the intentional design elements.

As a designer and a teacher of beading, I have to think about these ethics. While I'm learning a new stitch, I think about other possibilities for it. As soon as possible, I experiment with new ways to put the same stitch together or ways to combine it with something I already know. I try to work my way to a piece that looks significantly different from the one I learned from. Then I can feel the design is truly mine.

About these designs

My designs are the result of a lot of play, a lot of experimentation, and a whole lot of doing over and over again. Sometimes an idea will come quickly, and sometimes I have to work for it. Either way, I usually make a design several times, trying different variations of color or texture or shape before I'm satisfied.

Of course, I hope I haven't stepped on any design toes. There is so much going on in the bead world today, it's impossible to keep up with what every other designer is doing. Because we all work with the same beads and the same stitches, we're bound to come to similar design conclusions. Several times I've had an idea and before I could even write it down, there it was, already worked out and published in a magazine!

We have to learn our craft from somewhere, and all designs spring from the foundation built as the artist learned. I am grateful to all of the wonderful beaders who have put work into the world to share.

About the Stitches

I've used many basic beading stitches in this book: right-angle weave, ladder, herringbone, peyote, and brick stitch. As each stitch is introduced, I share the fundamentals of the stitch, including illustrations to make the project more accessible to beginners. If you begin a project and need help with a stitch, refer back to the project that first used it.

Cube beads and these stitches

Earrings, pins, and decorative items like stars and crosses need to be pretty rigid or they cease to look like what they are supposed to be. Cubes hold shapes like these very well. On the other hand, if cubes are worked too tightly, they can lock together so you can't even get your needle in to tie off or run out a tail. (Brick stitch is probably the worst offender here.) Proper tension is one solution for this, and I give suggestions in these projects for maintaining tension and where tightness can be a problem.

Other pieces like bracelets and necklaces need to drape and bend, so you don't want them to be rigid. A string or loop of cube beads will bend at awkward angles. Inserting round beads helps the strand drape nicely. This also helps when working with cubes in peyote stitch or on a loom.

St. Petersburg chain

Moving beyond the widely known and well-loved stitches, I based the majority of designs in this book on St. Petersburg chain. I learned this stitch by making a project from *Bead&Button* magazine, and soon began altering it and creating new designs.

Stories I've read connect St. Petersburg chain with a hard-to-find Russian book by Maya Anufrieva, known casually among beaders as "the white book." This book has two St. Petersburg chain projects, a simple chain and a leaf pattern. The book calls the stitch a "stair" or "step" chain, which makes sense because each four-bead box looks like a step in a flight of stairs.

The St. Petersburg label is often used for both the single as well as the double chain, which uses two chains in a mirror image with common center beads.

Just as I was learning this stitch, I discovered 1.5 mm and 2 mm cubes. I had made a pair of seed bead earrings using symmetrical St. Petersburg chains and was dismayed at how the earring wanted to fold up like one of those touch-me-not ferns. It didn't take me long to put cube beads and the St. Pete technique together.

This tendency to roll up is a weakness and may account for why we don't see many pieces in this stitch. The flat sides of the cube beads keep the St. Petersburg chain from rolling up. In fact, any stitch that tends to roll up in the direction of the roundness of seed beads will hold a shape better when made with cube beads.

Variations on St. Petersburg

I've used St. Petersburg chain as the starting point for many exciting designs in this book. Often, I spread the two sides of a symmetrical chain apart to insert other beadwork. In the Russian Waltz necklace, I use three beads in the center instead of one, opening up spaces in the chain for a lacy look. The evergreen, heart, and fan earrings are based on this idea of spread forms. To create a specific silhouette for some designs, I extend the arms to different lengths by adding beads.

And the most fun of all, I've attached several arms of the symmetrical chain around a ring of beads and joined them at the sides to make a series of points. This is the base of the medallion, star, snowflake, and cross designs. Once again, it is the cube beads that let these pieces hold their shape.

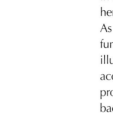

Bead Math

When I first started beading, it often puzzled me how to tell if I had enough beads to make a project. I didn't have a scale; most new beaders don't. My local shops didn't always include the gram weight (often abbreviated to "g") on the container of beads they sold me. I would wonder: Is this half-full tube of 11° beads enough for my project?

Here's a useful table of information based on the ubiquitous teaspoon. This method is not scientific, but practical. I arrived at these numbers by weighing and counting many samples of my own beads.

One level (though not obsessively so) teaspoon of the following beads equals between 7 and 7.5 g: 8°s, 11°s, 15°s, and 2 mm and 1.5 mm cubes. If your project calls for 14 g of any of these beads, two teaspoons should do the job. Extrapolating, a well-rounded quarter teaspoon yields about 2 g of any of these beads.

The quantity of beads in 1 g varies:
8°s: 37–42 beads
11°s: 110–120 beads
15°s: 250–260 beads
1.5 mm cubes: 100–110 beads
2 mm cubes: 48–52 beads

If you need 250 or 2 g of 11°s, two rounded teaspoons should do. An old set of measuring spoons has become a mainstay of my beading tool kit!

Bracelets

These bracelets introduce most of the stitches used in this book. You'll find that they all work up pretty fast, and each makes a nice addition to your bracelet wardrobe.

The Herringbone Classic bracelet is especially versatile and can be made in any of the four cube sizes. Stitched with 1.5 mm or 2 mm cubes, it can grace even the tiniest arm. I have a male friend who wears my herringbone bracelets made with larger cubes. If you like a cuff, the herringbone and peyote bracelets may be just your style. Make them as wide as you like simply by adding onto the width of the original design.

The last bracelet in this chapter, the Sunburst Medallion, introduces a technique that is used in the chapters on rings and decorative pendants. This technique builds a series of points in the St. Petersburg chain technique around a center ring of beads. Whether you're a beginner or advanced student of beading, I think you'll find this an exciting way to work St. Petersburg.

Squares Dancing

Herringbone Classic

Peyote Patterns

Willow Branch

Sunburst Medallion

I love the way the cubes play in this easy, right-angle weave piece. It makes an adorable little bracelet and a great anklet as well. Squares Dancing is a fun project to make for a child or a young girl. A beginning beader will appreciate its simplicity, so if you have a friend who wants to learn, this would make an excellent first piece to do together.

As a variation, consider adding dangles. For a sophisticated look, use tiny pearl seed beads with pearls as the drop bead or brilliant metallics with gold or silver drops.

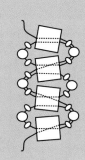

MATERIALS
For an 8¾ in. (22.2 cm) anklet or a shorter bracelet
- 32 3 mm cube beads
- 64 8º seed beads
- 2 g 11º seed beads
- Toggle clasp
- 5 mm soldered jump ring
- Beading thread
- 2 #10 beading needles

This version is anklet length. See how the cubes dance?

Technique

Right-angle weave

This simple bracelet or anklet is made using a chain of right-angle weave. Right-angle weave is often stitched in rings of four beads, where each bead sits at a right angle to the next. Additional bead rings are added by following a figure-8 path. Sometimes abbreviated to RAW, this stitch can also be worked in multiple rows.

In this bracelet, the central bead is a 3 mm cube, with a pattern of 11º, 8º, and 11º seed beads on both sides. The direction of the thread alternates as you weave in and out, pulling the tension alternately to one side and then the other. This is what makes the cube beads dance.

a

b

c

STEP 1 Fold 1½ yd. (1.4 m) of thread, leaving one tail about 6 in. (15 cm) long, and fasten the fold to the loop end of the clasp with a lark's head knot. Thread a needle on each end. Run both threads through an 8º bead. With the short tail, pick up four 11ºs. With the working thread, pick up four 11ºs and the cube bead, then go back through the four 11ºs that are on the short tail, through the 8º, through the jump ring and back through the 8º, the four 11ºs, and the cube bead [a]. The two tails should meet.

STEP 2 Tie the tails in a surgeon's knot. Run the long working thread back through the cube bead, and gently pull the knot into the cube bead behind it. Leave the short tail loose for now.

STEP 3 Pattern
Pick up this sequence on your needle: one each of an 11º, 8º, 11º, cube, 11º, 8º, and 11º. Go through the previous cube in the same direction as the first time. (The hole in the first cube bead should accommodate the knot and your needle.) Then go through the previous 11º, 8º, 11º, and cube bead. You will be coming out the cube in the opposite direction from the first pass [b].

STEP 4 Repeat the sequence in Step 3 until you are about ⅝ in. (1.6 cm) from the desired length. Work from your dominant side, turning the work after each step.

STEP 5 When your piece is ready to finish off, your thread should be coming out of a cube bead. Pick up five 11ºs, go through the clasp, and go back through the five 11ºs and the cube bead. From the other side of the cube, pick up three 11ºs, go through the two 11ºs nearest the clasp, through the clasp [c], and back through the same five seed beads and the cube bead.

STEP 6 Now you will need to tie off. (See page 13 for more information on finishing.) One option is to run the thread back a few rounds into the work and tie a series of half-hitch knots at several points in the work as you exit.

You can also create a second tail by passing the thread through the work in a circle so it comes back and meets itself, holding onto the loop the thread makes. Then you can tie the tail to the loop with a surgeon's knot. If you put your knot near a cube bead, you can gently pull the knot into the hole of the bead to hide it. Run both tails through a few more beads, and trim the thread close to the work.

To hide the tail you left at the beginning of the bracelet, run it through the work an inch or so, and trim.

Your bracelet or anklet is ready to wear!

Variations

Leafy look—Replace the 8º beads along one side with leaves or drops.

Add some dangles—Go back through the work with another thread and create dangles: Coming out a cube bead, pick up two 11º beads, a drop bead, an 11º, and go back through the dangle and the two 11ºs into the cube bead; repeat at intervals. If you plan ahead, you can add about 12 in. (30 cm) to your starting thread, turn around after you attach the second half of the clasp, add dangles as you work back to the other end, and tie the working thread to the original tail.

This anklet-size version uses pearl dangles (see instructions at left). Dangles can enhance a bracelet or a necklace too.

If you've never worked herringbone stitch, this is a great project to learn from, and you'll have a beautiful bracelet when you're done. The large beads make it easy for beginners, children, or those with bad eyesight to see how the stitch goes together, and the flat sides of the cubes help the beads lie in place without slipping around too much.

For the lover of wide cuffs, this bracelet is easily broadened to 8 or even 12 beads wide. When you build the beginning ladder, just keep adding beads until the piece is wide enough, always stopping with an even number of beads. You'll need a wider clasp, and I recommend a box clasp or a slide-lock clasp for the cuff-width bracelets.

Make a bolder narrow bracelet with 4 mm cube beads—you might even get your guy to wear this one! Or try the same design with 1.5 mm or 2 mm cubes for a delicate look. I've made these using a number of combinations, such as matte teal with glossy navy, matte black with iridescent gold, and matte purple with silver.

Technique

Ladder start for herringbone stitch

Building a ladder is a good basic technique to know. Working with cubes makes this much easier than with any kind of rounded bead.

To make a ladder, pick up two beads, go through the first bead again in the same direction, pull through to align the two beads side by side, and go through the second bead again in the same direction. * Pick up another bead, go through the previous bead in the same direction as before, align the new bead against the previous bead, and go through the new bead again in the same direction. Repeat from the * until you have the desired length. As you work, be sure to pull your thread taut so there is no space between beads.

Herringbone is a beautiful stitch. The pull of the thread as you stitch causes the beads to tilt alternately, creating a texture reminiscent of loomed herringbone fabric. This stitch often has a turnaround bead at the end of each row. When you get to the end of a row, you have to turn to work the next row in the opposite direction. If you go directly into the next bead, some thread will show. One way to hide the thread is to loop the thread through the edge beads, but I think that distorts the pattern along the edges. The version I've used here incorporates a turnaround bead (two beads, in fact) as part of the pattern.

At the end of each row, you will turn the work left to right and work back in the opposite direction. Here you will pick up the two turnaround beads, and go up into the last bead of the previous row. This will place you at the right point to begin a new row. After I add the two turnaround beads, place the first two beads in the row, and come up for the second set of beads, I take a moment to tighten the previous row (see Tip). Developing this habit will help you as you progress to wider pieces, because it's harder to take up slack when the row is six or more beads wide.

This illustration shows the ladder (black thread) and the first row of herringbone with two turnaround beads (red thread).

MATERIALS

- 150 3 mm cube beads in opaque khaki AB
- About 50 3 mm cube beads in dark metallic gold
- About 90 11º seed beads in dark metallic gold
- Toggle clasp
- Beading thread
- #10 beading needle

Add two or three rows to each side for a dramatic cuff.

TIP

Keeping even tension is one of the challenges of herringbone. It's especially challenging in a project like this, which uses beads with large holes and only a few beads to a row. Keep a firm hold on the thread, much as you would in crochet. Grasp the work in your nondominant hand between the thumb and forefinger. Wrap the thread over the end of the forefinger and then under and around the middle finger once or twice at the first knuckle. If you then bend the middle finger, you have a good grip on the thread, and you can adjust the tension by moving your forefinger up and down. This is especially important as you turn the work to begin the next row.

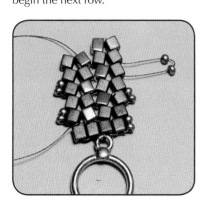

If you let the tension on your thread get sloppy, the work can become loose and uneven. Stop, put down the needle, get hold of the turnaround beads, and pull them away from the work. You will see the previous row tighten up. Pull the working thread to tighten up all the work, and you're ready to begin again.

a

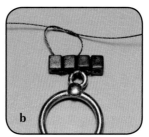
b

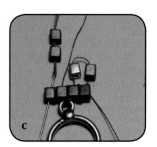
c

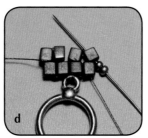
d

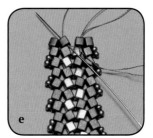
e

f

STEP 1 Thread a needle on 2½ yd. (2.3 m) of thread; this should be enough to finish the entire bracelet. Leaving a 6-in. (15 cm) tail, build a four-bead ladder with the khaki cube beads.

STEP 2 With the thread coming out the second bead from the end of the side opposite the tail, sew on the loop half of the clasp, alternately going in and out of the two center beads **[a]**. Come out the bead next to the tail, and tie the two ends with a surgeon's knot **[b]**. Bring the knot and working thread into the second bead from the right and back up the end bead on the side opposite the clasp. Leave the tail loose for now.

STEP 3 Pattern
Always work from your dominant side (the right if you are right-handed). Pick up a khaki and a dark gold cube bead, and pass the needle down through the cube next to the one you have come out of and back up the next cube. Pull the thread through. Pick up two khaki cubes, and pass down

through the last cube in the previous row **[c]**. This is one herringbone row.

Turn the work so that you are working from the opposite direction. Pick up two 11ºs, and pass up through the first cube in the previous row **[d]**. Pick up a khaki and a dark gold cube, and go down through the second cube and up through the third cube in the previous row. Pick up two khaki cubes, and go down through the last cube in the previous row. This is the second herringbone row. Repeat this row until you have completed the length you need.

The placement of the gold 11ºs will reverse each time you turn your work, so the pattern will alternate even though you use the same order of beads in each row.

STEP 4 Ending
The last row will be similar to the first. Using only the khaki cubes in the last row, pass back in circles through the last four cubes, pulling them closer together as in

the original ladder **[e]**. Bring the thread out one of the center cubes going away from the work. Pick up three khaki cubes, pass through the ring of the toggle half of the clasp, back through the three cubes and into the adjacent cube in the last row **[f]**. Make this pass two or three times. Work the tail back into the last few rows, tie off, and trim.

Note: It's important to tie a knot in the ends because herringbone stitch is quite flexible and the holes in the cube beads are fairly large. Tails that just run through the work will loosen.

Weave in the loose tail that you left at the beginning.

Metallic accents

I like to put a little gold or silver in my designs. This helps my beaded work blend well with other jewelry. Many people prefer either gold or silver and find their skin tone goes better with one or the other.

You'll want to watch out for metal coatings that rub off. An easy test is to splash a bit of nail polish remover on a clean, white tissue and rub the bead firmly. If color comes off onto the tissue, the finish won't last long on the arm. Often, metal coatings are put onto black or dark bases, and a worn bead can look badly discolored.

When you're buying, look for metallic beads marked "permanent." Don't hesitate to ask if coatings are permanent and return them if they turn out not to be.

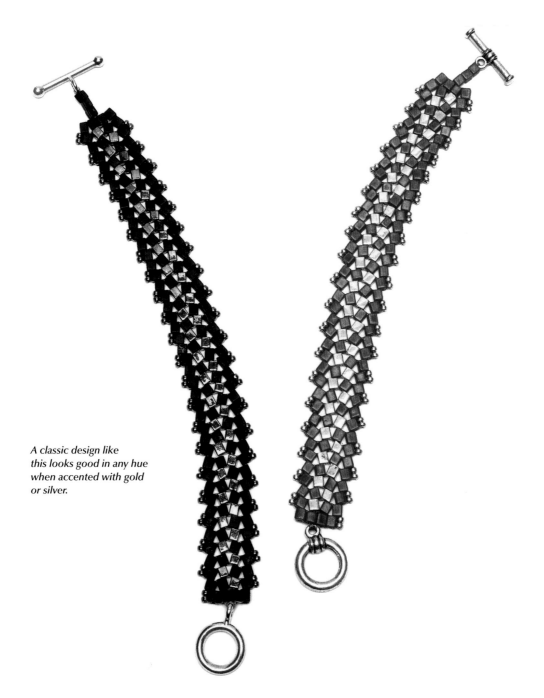

A classic design like this looks good in any hue when accented with gold or silver.

Peyote stitch is not that hard, and it's a versatile stitch to know. Also called gourd stitch, it was used widely by Native American beaders. It's no wonder the patterns that arise naturally when you work this stitch look like native work. The stitch is a natural for patterns that feature diagonals and triangles.

I like beading with repeating patterns. I get a mantra to follow and a free meditation session, yet I'm forced to pay attention. It's easy when doing long projects to drift into lazy work. When you make a patterned piece, your mistakes are visible for all to see!

Technique

Peyote stitch

Starting is the hardest part of peyote. If you can make it through the first four passes, you're on your way!

Peyote can be stitched with one, two, or three beads at a time. For two-drop peyote, instead of working with one bead at a time, you pick up two, skip two and go through two.

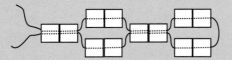

This bracelet uses a mix; the edges are two-drop, and the center is one-drop. This mix of technique allows the development of the diagonal striped pattern in the center section. At the same time, it allows the placement of the 3 mm cube along the edge, which is double the size of the 1.5 mm and substitutes for two of them.

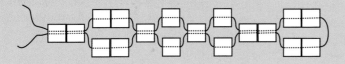

MATERIALS
- **About 20 3 mm cubes**
- **14 g each 1.5 mm cubes in colors A, B, and C**
- **Box clasp**
- **Beading thread**
- **#10 beading needle**

TIP Try to work taut. If you lose the tension in your work, you can take it up by pulling the first pair of beads in the row you just made away from the work. This will tighten up the previous row. Then take out the slack in the row you just made. You can back up a few rows, taking out the slack sequentially in the order you made the rows.

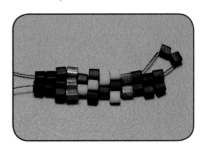

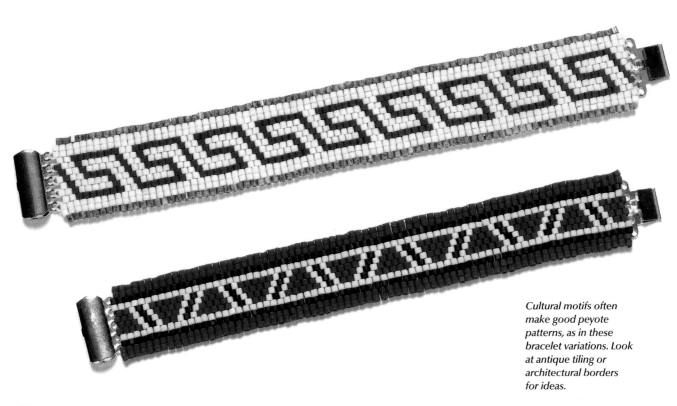

Cultural motifs often make good peyote patterns, as in these bracelet variations. Look at antique tiling or architectural borders for ideas.

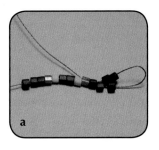

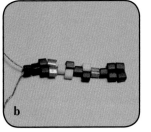

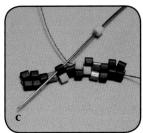

STEP 1 Thread a needle on 2 yd. (1.8 m) of thread.

STEP 2 Pick up 3A, 1B, 1C, 2A, 1C, 1B, and 3A. Turn. Pick up 2A, skip 2A, go through 1A and 1B **[a]**. Pick up 1A, skip 1C, go through 1A. Pick up 1 C, skip 1A, go through 1C. Pick up 1B and 1A, skip 1B and 1A, go through 2A.

This finishes the first three rows. Pull the beads taut, and be sure they are lying in their right relationships **[b]**. Turn so both ends are coming out the right side with your working thread farthest from you. From this position, you will work back across the last row.

STEP 3 Fourth row
Pick up 2A, skip 2A, go through 1A and 1B. Pick up 1A, skip 1C, go through 1C. Pick up 1C, skip 1A, go through 1A **[c]**. Pick up 1B and 1A, skip 1B and 1A, go through 2A.

STEP 4 Pattern
This is a pretty easy pattern if you just follow the rules.

First step: Always pick up two As, skip two As, and go through the pair of one A and one B.

Middle: Always pick up the opposite color of the one in the dip **[d]**. If you pick up an A the first time, the next cube you pick up will be a C.

Last step: Always pick up a B and an A, skip a B and an A, and go through two A. This finishes a row.

Turn and repeat.

STEP 5 3 mm cube
This pattern changes only to add the 3 mm. When you have finished 10 rows (count five beads on each edge) and gone back through the last pair a second time, add a 3 mm in place of the pair of As **[e]**. Then continue adding pairs of As as usual **[f]**. The 3 mm will create a slight wave in the edge.

In this piece, two chains of St. Petersburg stitch mirror each other. At the center of the pattern is a large cube bead that ties the chains together as you pass through the cube from both sides. The Willow Leaf earrings on page 42 use a similar technique and make great matching earrings.

When it's created with round seed beads, this stitch tends to fold up along the center line. The cubes help it hold its shape. This can be a delicate bracelet made with 1.5 mm cubes and 3 mm centers, or you can beef it up by pairing 2 mm and 4 mm cubes.

MATERIALS

- About 30 3 mm cubes in metallic or contrasting color
- 14 g 1.5 mm matte gray cube beads
- About 60 11º seed beads to match 3 mm cubes
- Toggle clasp
- Beading thread
- 2 #10 beading needles

Notice the difference when the bracelet is made with 1.5 mm and 3 mm cubes (left) or 2 mm and 4 mm cubes (right).

Technique

St. Petersburg double chain

The St. Petersburg double chain is two simple chains in a symmetrical relationship, joined at their center by one or several beads. (To see a simple chain, look at the Rainbow Lariat project on page 60.)

STEP 1 The first step in St. Pete is to arrange two beads alongside two previous beads to form a box. I call the two beads pulled alongside the *return beads* (shown in blue in fig. 1). In this example, you would pick up six beads, and count to the fourth and third beads away from the needle. Go through the fourth and third beads again, in the same direction as before, and align the last two beads you picked up against the previous two beads, creating a box of four beads.

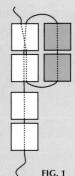

FIG. 1

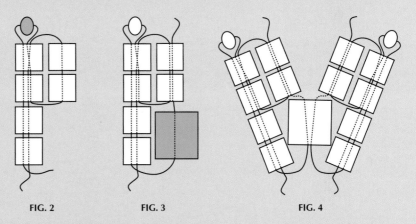

FIG. 2   FIG. 3   FIG. 4

STEP 2 Next you will add a bead before you go back into the same bead you just exited so the thread does not just pull through. I call this bead the *turnaround bead* (in blue, fig. 2). Go back through two beads, and then go through two more beads below the box. This allows the center bead, which is usually double the size of the smaller beads, to fit into the space you've made.

STEP 3 Pick up the center bead (in blue, fig. 3), and go through the two return beads. This completes one sequence, which you will continue to repeat on the first side.

STEP 4 On the second side, you will follow the same steps, except instead of adding a center bead, you will go through the center bead of the first side [fig. 4].

When I'm teaching this stitch, I usually have my students alternate the sequence, as in the instructions for this bracelet project, so they have the experience of putting the two sides together. However, if your work is going well and you wish to work faster, you can complete an entire side of the double chain, adding the center beads along the way, then come back to where you left off to finish the other side. Remember to go through the center beads that are already in the first side.

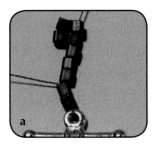

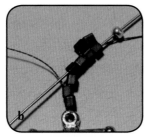

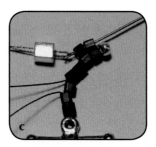

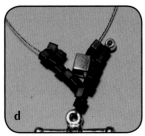

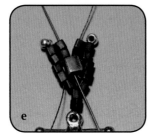

Ways to speed up St. Petersburg chain

A lot of the pieces in this book use St. Petersburg chain as a base. It's a useful and pretty stitch worth practicing. Here are some tips I've found that make the work go easier and faster.

• After you pick up the turnaround bead and go through the four beads below it, continue through the center bead and the return beads before you pull the thread through. The holes in cube beads are large enough to let you do this without stressing the thread, especially if you are using a strong line like Power Pro.

• The stitch goes quickly if you hold it in your hand like crochet. I often work with the emerging piece held between thumb and forefinger and the working thread wrapped around my middle finger for tension. If I pull up the first five beads of the pattern and lay them over my forefinger with the tail wrapped, they are in perfect position to find the fourth and third beads without having to fish for them.

Note: The extra cubes you'll add in Steps 1 and 3 give the toggle flexibility. The pattern begins with Step 2 and continues in Step 4.

STEP 1 Fold 3 yd. (2.7 m) of thread in half. Attach to the toggle end of the clasp with a lark's head knot. Thread a needle on each end, and pick up two 1.5 mm cube beads on both threads. Pick up two 1.5 mms on the right-hand thread.

STEP 2 Pattern, right side
Pick up five 1.5 mms, and go through the fourth and third bead from the needle again to form a box of four beads **[a]**. The two beads that turn back are the return beads. Pick up an 11º, and go back through the four cubes behind it **[b]**. This creates the turnaround bead. Pick up a

3 mm and go through the two return beads **[c]**.

STEP 3 Pick up two 1.5 mms on the left-hand thread.

STEP 4 Pattern, left side
This is a mirror of the right side. With the left-hand thread, pick up five 1.5 mms, and go through the fourth and third beads from the needle again, forming a box of four beads with two return beads **[d]**. Pick up an 11º, and go back through the four beads below it. Then take the thread through the 3 mm on the first side of the work and on through the return beads on the current side of the work **[e]**. This pulls the two sides together.

Note: At this point, it is a good idea to snug everything up. By pulling the turnaround beads away from the work,

you will take up any slack. Then pull the thread to take the slack out of the turnaround beads. This is a good practice to keep up as you go, especially if you are new to beading or if your work tends to be loose.

STEP 5 Repeat Step 2 and Step 4, starting with five 1.5 mms on each side, until you reach the desired length. If you prefer, do all of the right side, and then go back and do all of the left side.

STEP 6 Finishing
Sew the two sets of return beads together from both sides **[f]**. Sew the loop half of the clasp onto these beads **[g]**. Tie a surgeon's knot at the loop side of the 3 mm, and pull the knot into the 3 mm. Run the tails out into the work for an inch (2.5 cm) or two, and trim.

Sunburst Medallion

Do you have a favorite timepiece whose band has grown a bit tired? This dramatic look combines bead stitching with either a watch face or a lovely, large gemstone bead. Try a carved gemstone—a flower or scarab, for example—as your featured stone.

St. Petersburg gets a little more complex here. The first part of this bracelet is making the medallion center. This is done by attaching a series of arms around a center ring of 11º beads. Each section is attached to the previous one in a sequence that works its way around to the sides. A watch face or stone takes center stage, with a band made exactly like the Willow Branch bracelet on each side. You may want this bracelet to fit snug on the arm so it won't slip around.

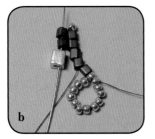

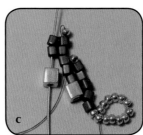

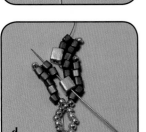

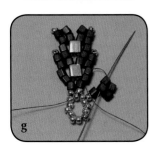

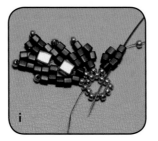

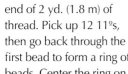

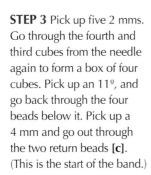

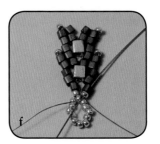

MATERIALS
- 14 g 4 mm cube beads
- 14 g 2 mm cube beads
- Matching 11º seed beads
- 16–20 mm watch face or flat-back gemstone
- 3-hole clasp
- Beading thread
- 4 #10 beading needles

TIP If you didn't make the Willow Branch bracelet, you may want to review the basics of St. Petersburg chain on page 29 before you start this project.

STEP 1 Center circle
Thread a needle on each end of 2 yd. (1.8 m) of thread. Pick up 12 11ºs, then go back through the first bead to form a ring of beads. Center the ring on the thread. You will have two threads coming off the ring with one bead between them.

STEP 2 Long arms Using either thread, pick up an 11º and seven 2 mm cubes. Go through the fourth and third beads from the needle again to form a box of four cubes **[a]**. The two beads that turn back are the return beads. Pick up an 11º, and go back through the four beads below it. Pick up a 4 mm, then go out through the two return beads **[b]**.

STEP 3 Pick up five 2 mms. Go through the fourth and third cubes from the needle again to form a box of four cubes. Pick up an 11º, and go back through the four beads below it. Pick up a 4 mm and go out through the two return beads **[c]**. (This is the start of the band.)

STEP 4 Repeat Steps 2 and 3 with the other thread, but use the same center 4 mms already in the first two arms **[d]**. When you have finished repeating, bring each thread back to the center ring of 11ºs by coming down the outside arms, through the 4 mm **[e]**, and over and down the beginning 2 mm and 11º **[f]**. Take both threads into the original ring and over one bead, so you are coming out the spaces to the sides of the starting space.

STEP 5 First side arm
Pick up an 11º and five 2 mms, and go through the fourth and third beads from the needle again. Rotate the return beads away from the long arm. Attach the top two 2 mms (not the return beads) to the adjacent two 2 mms in the long arm **[g]**. Pick up a 2 mm and an 11º, and go back through the 2 mm you just picked up and the two 2 mms and the 11º below it **[h]**. Then go through the 11º next over in the ring.

STEP 6 Second side arm
Pick up an 11º and five 2 mms. Go through the fourth and third beads again, and rotate the return beads toward the arm just made. * Pick up a 2 mm and an 11º, go back through the 2 mm just picked up and the two 2 mms below it **[i]**. Go up through the

This muted palette of gray, blue, and brown sets off the silver watch and blends beautifully with almost any wardrobe.

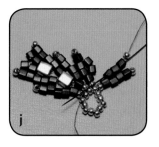

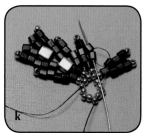

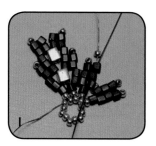

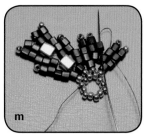

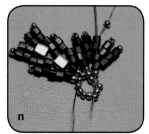

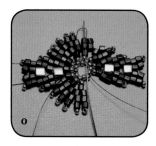

two return beads. Pick up a 2 mm and an 11º, and go back through the 2 mm just picked up and the two return beads [j]. Attach the bottom new return bead (your thread is coming out of it) to the bottom return bead in the last arm you made. Go out the second return bead [k]. Pick up a 2 mm and an 11º. Go back through the 2 mm you just picked up and the 2 mm below that [l].

STEP 7 Now you'll add a short half-arm to fill the gap between the first and second side arms. Pick up a 2 mm, and attach it to the 2 mm you just came out, then similarly attach the new 2 mm to the 2 mm in the adjacent side arm [m].

(You may have to help this bead fit evenly between the other two. Push the beads into the placement you want, and tug gently a couple of times on the thread to take out the slack.) Pick up a 2 mm and an 11º. Go back through the 2 mm just picked up, the 2 mm below it, the next-lowest 2 mm, and the 2 mm and 11º of the second side arm [n]. You are back at the original ring.

STEP 8 Changing to the other thread, repeat Steps 5, 6, and 7 to make the side arms on the other side. When you are done, you will have finished half the center medallion.

STEP 9 Opposite side
Center a new 2-yd. (1.8 m) thread through the bead opposite the starting bead in the ring. Repeat the entire first half of the center section, Steps 2–8, except at the * of Step 6. Here, attach the two 2 mms you are coming out to the adjacent two 2 mms of the arm of the first side [o]. Then, continue to repeat Steps 6–8 until you have finished the medallion.

Note: If you are adding a stone bead instead of a watch face, refer to the instructions under "Option" on the next page.

STEP 10 Watch face

To begin adding a watch face, work the threads so they are coming out the ends of the long arms [p].

STEP 11 Side bands

Extend the long arms to the desired lengths using this pattern: Pick up five 2 mms, and go through the fourth and third cubes again. Pick up an 11º and go through the four beads below it. Pick up a 4 mm, (or if you are on the mirror side, the same 4 mm you used in the first side), and go through the two return beads.

STEP 12
Attaching a clasp

When your bracelet is the desired length, sew on a clasp. For a two-hole clasp, sew each thread to one ring of the clasp. For a three-hole clasp, sew each thread to the outside rings of the clasp. Attach a 2 mm cube between the two sets of return beads, and use it to attach the center ring of the clasp.

STEP 13
Attaching the watch face

Thread a new length of strong or doubled thread on a needle, center the watch face, and stitch it to the medallion. You may need to add a few seed beads to hide the thread [q]. Make several passes for security. To tie off, make a knot in the center back of the medallion so you can find it easily when you need to undo it to replace the battery. Don't glue the knot. Run 1–2-in. (2.5–5 cm) tails out toward the band.

OPTION

To add a focal gemstone bead instead of a watch face, skip Step 10, insert the following step before you do Step 11, and skip Step 13.

Work the four threads back through the ring and out the 11º and 2 mms on each long side.

Use 11ºs on each side of the focal bead to center it. The two threads from one side will cross the other two in the focal bead. Leaving the focal bead and its adjusting beads, go into the same beads you came out on the opposite sides, and go all the way through the long arms of the piece until you come out the two center 2 mms at the ends of the long arms.

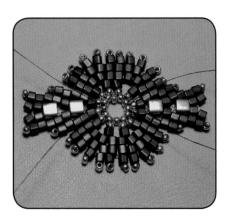

Instead of a watch face, highlight a multicolored gemstone or a beautiful carved flower or scarab. Accentuate the subtle colors of the focal point with your bead selection.

Earrings

One of the easiest ways to learn a stitch is by making earrings. These are short projects, and starting over (should you need to) isn't a big deal. The earring projects offer a wide range of techniques and styles. The last few designs in this chapter are fairly complex, but if you start at the beginning and work your way through these earrings in sequence, by the time you get to the complex ones, you'll be quite familiar with the techniques, and they will seem much easier.

Many of these earrings have shapes that are universal in appeal, like the diamond, hexagon, evergreen, heart, and fan. They can be changed in scale by switching to larger or smaller cube beads. They can be made into dangles, drops, pendants, and decorations. They can be strung together or used as elements in other pieces of jewelry. They can be glued onto things like decorated boxes or sculptures. They can be sewed onto jackets and dresses and shirts or incorporated into bead embroidery.

I wear earrings more than any other jewelry, so I'm always trying out new designs. When I go to lunch with my friends, they're often eyeing my ears to see what new earrings I'm wearing. These are so much fun, I've given them for gifts myself.

Ladder & Loops

Brick Stitch
Geometrics

Willow Leaves

Russian Drops

Evergreens

Light Hearts

Spanish Fans

These earrings illustrate two things about cube beads. Cube beads make very stable, even stiff, ladders. And, if you want to shape cubes into a circle, add the "grease" of a round bead between each one.

You can use almost any combination for the ladder and the loops as long as the cubes in the ladder are just as large as, or larger than, the cubes in the loops. There are a lot of variations on this simple base. Make a stack of loops, add drops to your loops, try an S-shape, or overlap two figure-8s.

Technique

Two-needle ladder stitch

We built a ladder in the herringbone bracelet earlier in this book with one threaded needle. These earrings start with a ladder stitch that uses two threaded needles. To work in ladder stitch, pass each needle through a cube from opposite directions, crossing the threads in the bead and pulling tight. Your ladder should be solid and straight. With cube beads, this is so easy—the large, flat-sided beads behave perfectly.

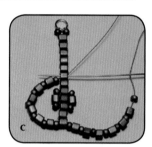

MATERIALS
- **60 2 mm cube beads**
- **50 11º seed beads**
- **2 small soldered jump rings**
- **Pair of earring findings**
- **Beading thread**
- **2 #10 or #12 beading needles**

This simple design lends itself to many variations. Double the figure-8 …

… or use tiny drops for a flowery effect.

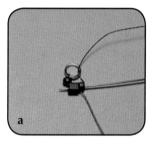
a

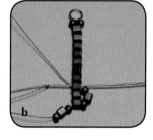
b

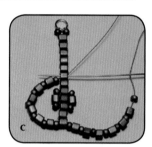
c

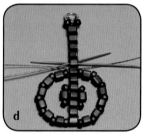
d

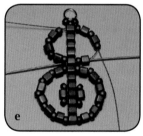
e

STEP 1 Thread a needle on each end of 1 yd. (.9 m) of thread. Pick up an 11º seed bead, a cube bead, and an 11º with one needle, and center the group of beads on the thread. Go through a jump ring with each needle and then back through the nearest 11º and the cube **[a]**. The threads will cross in the cube.

STEP 2 Using two-needle ladder stitch, add nine cubes to create a ladder of 10 cubes.

STEP 3 Pick up an 11º, a cube, and an 11º with each needle, and cross the needles through the eighth cube in the ladder **[b]**. Cross again in the ninth and tenth cubes. Add two more cubes to the ladder for a total of 12 cubes.

STEP 4 On one needle, pick up an 11º and a cube six times. Pick up one more 11º, and go through the sixth cube. Repeat on the other side **[c]**. Run one thread back through the entire circle just made for stability, coming back out the same place you started. Cross both threads in the next cube up **[d]**.

STEP 5 On one needle, pick up an 11º and a cube three times. Pick up one more 11º, and go through the first cube. Repeat on the other side. Run one thread through the opposite half-circle **[e]**. Repeat on the other side. Tie off.

STEP 6 Attach the earring finding to the jump ring.

STEP 7 Make a second earring to match the first.

Learn brick stitch while you make a pair of lovely diamond or hexagon earrings. Although brick stitch is usually rigid in one direction, cube beads help these earrings hold their open shape in both directions. In fact, they can support a drop or pearl dangling from the tip or the open center without losing their shape. These are so easy and versatile, you can make a pair in every color you like!

Experiment with cube size. Be bold with 2 mm cubes or dainty with 1.5 mm cubes. Once you have the earrings down, try linking the shapes with simple St. Petersburg chain for a modern necklace.

MATERIALS
Brick Stitch Diamonds
- **14 g each 2 mm cube beads in colors A and B**
- **2 15° seed beads to match color A**
- **2 small soldered jump rings**
- **Pair of earring findings**
- **Strong beading thread such as Power Pro or Fireline**
- **#10 or #12 beading needle**

Elongate the shape with a bottom dangle.

TIP You want the earring to hold its shape, but it's possible to pull this piece so tight that you can't get your needle into it to tie off. You want to take out the slack at every stitch, but don't pull too hard on the thread.

If you make this earring with 1.5 mm cubes instead of 2 mms, you may want to change to a #12 needle and thinner thread. It's easy to break a bead with this tight stitch.

Technique

Brick stitch

Brick stitch starts with a row of ladder stitch. The ladder in this project is made with one thread.

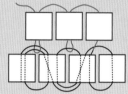

Brick stitch builds like a wall of bricks, so every bead is offset by half the width of the bead below. Each bead is attached to the thread that runs between the two beads below it. You want to try to catch the entire thread or threads when you run your needle under them.

Because each bead is offset from the one below it, every row either increases or decreases by half a bead width. These earrings use this angled edge to create the sides of the geometric shapes.

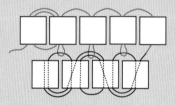

You'll need to know how to decrease and increase. In a row that decreases on the beginning edge, you should be coming up out the second bead from the end. In a row that decreases on the finishing edge, you will stop before you add a bead that overhangs the edge.

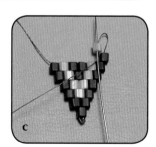

In a row that increases on the beginning edge, you should be coming up out the last bead from the end. In a row that increases on the finishing edge, you must add a bead using a ladder stitch, because there is no thread to attach the bead to.

Often you will end a row and not be in position to start the next row. You may need to take the thread in and out of a few beads to maneuver to the right place. In these instructions, I tell when you need to do this and what route to take.

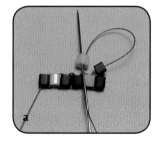
a

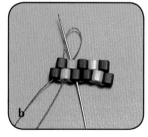
b

c

Diamonds
To make this earring, you'll start just below center, work down to the bottom point, up each side, and to the top.

STEP 1 Bottom point
Thread a needle with 4 ft. (1.2 m) of thread, leaving an 18-in. (46 cm) tail. Make a ladder with the working thread using cube beads in this order: A, B, A, A, B, A. After you finish the ladder, go back through the second cube from the needle. You will be coming out of a B bead on the opposite side from the tail.

STEP 2 Pick up an A and B, and attach the B with brick stitch **[a]**. Then stitch an A, B, and A. To get into position for another decrease row, go down into the work and back out the second bead from the edge **[b]**. Turn.

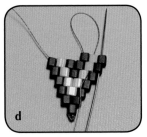

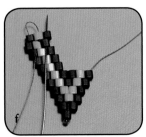

Stitch a small jump ring into the top of the opening, and hang a dangle from it.

STEP 3 Third row
Stitch an A, B, B, and A. Turn.

STEP 4 Fourth row
Stitch an A, B, and A. Turn.

STEP 5 Fifth row
Stitch two As. Turn.

STEP 6 Point
Turn the work right side up, so the tip is pointing downward. Pick up an A and a 15º. Go back through the A you picked up and through the A to the right of the one you started from. Continue through the work, coming out the outside bead on the first row on the side opposite the tail.

Your working thread should be on your right (or dominant) side. You will increase outward along only one side, so you will always start a new row by coming up out the last bead to the right of the previous row (see Technique, page 39).

STEP 7 First side
Pick up an A and a B, and attach B as before [c]. Then stitch an A. Go down through the adjacent B and the B below it, then go up through the adjacent A and the A above [d]. Turn. Repeat this row three times for a total of four rows. On the last row, do not go down into the work, but turn the work and increase for four rows toward the inside [e]. Go down into the work to get in position for the next four rows also [f].

STEP 8 Second side
Thread a needle on the tail and use it to repeat the first side, increasing outward from the center for four rows and increasing inward toward the center for four rows. Your final two rows should meet in the middle. Join them using the original thread [g]. Work across to come out the second bead from the end.

STEP 9 Top point
Repeat the steps for building the bottom, decreasing on both sides and following the same pattern [h]. When you reach the next-to-last row of two A cubes, stitch them together. Attach a jump ring to them, going out of one bead, through the jump ring, and back into the same bead [i]. Repeat with the other bead. Do this twice if you can. Work the two ends toward each other. Tie off, and trim.

Note: The work will be quite tight as you go to tie off, and you may need to bend it to get the needle in and out. If you're working with 1.5 mm cubes, a few half hitches or directional changes in the thread path will do. If you're working with 2 mm cubes, try to tie a surgeon's knot.

STEP 10 Attach the earring finding to the earring.

STEP 11 Make a second earring to match the first.

OPTIONS

If you want to add a drop at the bottom, pick it up instead of the 15º in Step 6. Or you can attach a soldered jump ring at the top of the center opening, then hang a drop from the jump ring using a head pin and loop.

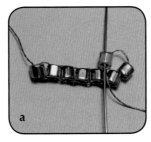

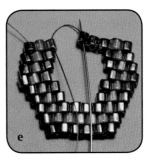

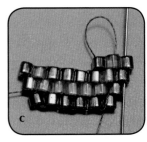

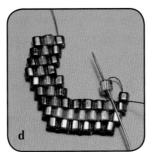

MATERIALS
Brick Stitch Hexagons
- 14 g each 2 mm cube beads in colors A and B
- 2 small soldered jump rings
- Pair of earring findings
- Strong beading thread such as Power Pro or Fireline
- #10 beading needle

Create longer, dramatic earrings with a few extra beads and some simple wirework loops.

Hexagons

STEP 1 Bottom
Thread a needle on 1¼ yd. (1.1 m) of thread, leaving an 18-in. (46 cm) tail. Using color A beads, build a six-bead ladder. Your thread should be coming out the last bead on the row. Turn. (If this row starts to loosen, just take up the slack and move on.)

STEP 2
Pick up one A and one B, and attach the B with brick stitch as shown [a]. This creates an increase at the beginning of the row. Pick up and stitch four Bs. Pick up an A, and attach it to the last B with ladder stitch. This creates an increase at the end of the row. Take the thread in and out of the work so you are coming out the last bead in the last row [b]. You are in position to increase again. Turn.

STEP 3
Pick up an A and a B, and attach as before. Pick up and stitch four As. Pick up and stitch a B. Pick up one A and attach it to the last B. Turn as in Step 2.

STEP 4 First side
Pick up an A and B, and attach the B as before. Stitch one A. Take the thread down the adjacent B and the B below it, then up through the adjacent A and the A above it [c]. You are in position to increase again on the outside edge. Repeat this row twice, but on the last row, do not go down into the work, but turn it so you are working in the opposite direction.

STEP 5
Repeat the previous three rows, but increase toward the center.

STEP 6 Second side
Thread a needle on the tail. It should be coming out the last bead on the row. You are now in position to increase. Repeat Steps 4 and 5 to finish the second side [d].

STEP 7 Joining
Using the original thread, join the final row on each side by adding two A beads between them with ladder stitch [e]. Work across the row so the thread comes out the next-to-last bead in the row.

STEP 8 Top
From here on, you will be decreasing, which means you will always want to come out the next-to-last bead in the row [f]. Stitch one A, five Bs, and one A. This row will be centered over the previous row. Work the thread in and out of the beads so you are again coming out the next-to-last bead in the row.

STEP 9
Work a row of six As. Sew on a jump ring using the two center beads of the last row [g]. Tie off.

STEP 10
Attach an earring finding.

STEP 11
Make a second earring to match the first.

This project is excellent for those new to St. Petersburg double chain. (For a refresher on the stitch, see page 29.) Earrings work up quickly, and the cube beads hold the leaf shape so it doesn't fold up, yet the pattern is flexible and swings beautifully.

If you like delicate, dangly earrings, these are for you. Make them as dramatically long as you want. These work especially well in any spring green or rich autumn combination. I also like the contemporary look of silver cubes marching down the length of the pretty aqua variation. For a different look, stitch a shorter earring, and add a drop or pearl at the bottom.

MATERIALS
- 14 g 1.5 mm cube beads
- 14 3 mm cube beads
- 34 11° seed beads
- 2 small soldered jump rings
- Pair of earring findings
- Beading thread
- 2 #10 beading needles

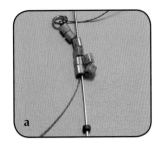

a

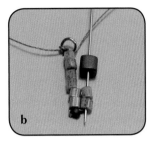

b

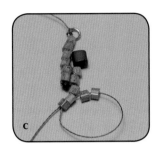

c

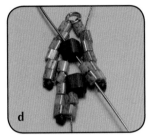

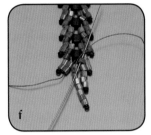

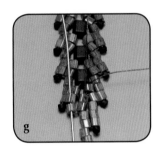

d

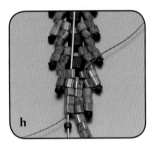

e

f

g

h

An odd number of cubes works well in these— try three, five, or seven. A drop or a pearl is a nice finish.

STEP 1 Fold 1 yd. (.9 m) of thread in half, and attach the loop end to a jump ring with a lark's head knot. Thread a needle on each end.

STEP 2 Pick up eight 1.5 mm cube beads, and go through the fourth and third cubes from the needle again to form a box of four beads.

STEP 3 Pick up an 11°, and go back up four of the six cubes above it **[a]**. Pick up a 3 mm cube, and go down through the two return beads **[b]**.

STEP 4 Pick up five 1.5 mms. Go through the fourth and third beads from the needle again as before **[c]**. Pick up an 11°, and go back up the four beads above it. Pick up a 3 mm, and go down through the two return beads.

STEP 5 Repeat Steps 2–4 on the other side using the other needle, but use the 3 mms already in place **[d]**.

STEP 6 Repeat the pattern on both sides, tying the two sides together by running through the same 3 mm in the center. Work until your earring is the desired length.

STEP 7 To finish the tip of the leaf, pick up five 1.5 mms, and go through the fourth and third beads from the needle again. Pick up an 11°, and go back through the four beads above it. Pick up two 1.5 mms, and go down through the two return beads **[e]**. Pick up three 1.5 mms and an 11°, and go back up the seven cubes, the 1.5 mm in the adjacent arm, and come out under the 3 mm at the center **[f]**.

This row will create the center point of the leaf.

STEP 8 With the other thread, pick up a 1.5 mm, and attach it and the 1.5 mm above it to the adjacent two 1.5 mms in the center point row of the leaf **[g]**.

STEP 9 Pick up two 1.5 mms, and attach them in the same manner to the adjacent two 1.5 mms in the center point of the leaf, coming out downward. Pick up an 11°, and go back up the five beads above it **[h]**. Both threads should be coming out upward directly under the lowest 3 mm.

STEP 10 Tie the ends together under the 3 mm, pull the knot into the cube, run the tails out into the work for about an inch (2.5 cm), and trim.

STEP 11 Attach an earring finding.

STEP 12 Make a second earring to match the first.

These earrings start out like the Willow Leaves, but they incorporate little fringe drops on double loops. The drops have enough angle on their sides to allow the circle of cubes to bend. Lit from behind, these drops take on a lovely candlelight glow. I call them Russian because their base is St. Petersburg chain, and they have an elegant look, suitable for a czarina.

MATERIALS
- 2 g 1.5 mm cube beads
- 6 3 mm oval faceted beads
- 30 small fringe drops (2–3 mm)
- 2 2 mm soldered jump rings
- Pair of earring findings
- Beading thread
- 2 #10 beading needles

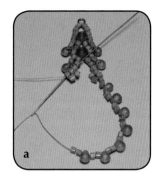

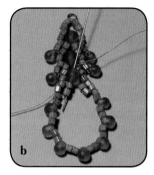

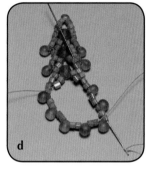

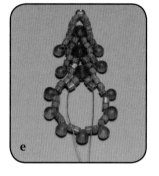

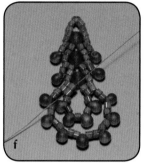

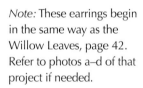

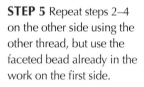

Experiment with color and placement. Against ivory, the faceted gold beads stand out. In the pair below, the brilliant green drops pop.

Note: These earrings begin in the same way as the Willow Leaves, page 42. Refer to photos a–d of that project if needed.

STEP 1 Fold 1 yd. (.9 m) of thread in half, and attach the loop end to one of the jump rings with a lark's head knot. Thread a needle on each end.

STEP 2 Pick up eight 1.5 mm cubes. Go through the fourth and third cubes from the needle again to form a box of four beads.

STEP 3 Pick up a drop, and go back up four of the cubes above it. Pick up a faceted bead and go down through the two return beads.

STEP 4 Pick up five cubes. Go through the fourth and third beads from the needle again as before. Pick up a drop, and go back through the four beads above it. Pick up a faceted bead, and go down through the return beads.

STEP 5 Repeat steps 2–4 on the other side using the other thread, but use the faceted bead already in the work on the first side.

STEP 6 Pick up five cubes, and go back through the fourth and third beads from the needle. Repeat with the other thread.

STEP 7 With either thread, pick up two cubes, one drop seven times, plus two cubes. Go up the four beads on the outside of the box on the opposite side **[a]**. Pick up one faceted bead and go down through the return beads on the first side **[b]**.

STEP 8 With the other thread, go back through the loop of cubes and drops in the opposite direction (be careful not to miss a bead!) **[c]**. Go up through the four cubes **[d]** and down through the faceted bead and the two return beads to mirror the track of the first thread. You have finished

the outer loop, and each of your threads will be coming down the lowest return beads on both sides **[e]**.

STEP 9 With either thread, pick up a cube and a drop four times plus a cube, and go up through the return beads on the opposite side **[f]**. You may need to adjust the number of beads on the inner loop so it fits nicely within the outer loop. Repeat with the other thread so that both threads are coming up the lowest return beads under the lowest faceted center bead.

STEP 10 Tie the ends together, pull the knot up into the faceted center bead, run the tails out into the work for about an inch (2.5 cm), and trim.

STEP 11 Attach an earring finding.

STEP 12 Make a second earring to match the first.

This is the project that sparked many of the designs in this book. I had made a St. Petersburg double chain bracelet with matte metallic green cubes, and the edge kept making me think that these beads and this stitch would make a great Christmas tree. It took many tries to get to these earrings, and they were the starting point for much creativity.

This use of St. Petersburg double chain spreads the two simple chains apart to insert several 3 mm cubes. You'll want to make these on a flat surface and you will definitely need a strong thread like Power Pro because you will be putting a lot of tension on it. You may need to "manhandle" the beads a bit to get them to lie in place until you can draw the tension up.

Worked in Christmas colors, these are fun earrings to wear at holiday events or to give as gifts, but you can make them in other colors like ivory and wear them year-round. Make a larger decorative evergreen with 2 mm and 4 mm cubes, and consider adding a sterling silver star to its peak.

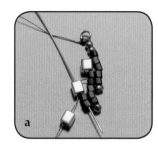

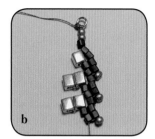

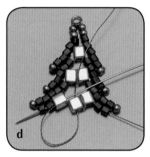

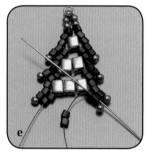

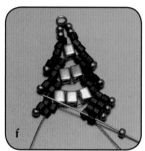

MATERIALS
- 12 3 mm cube beads
- 95 1.5 mm cube beads
- 36 11º seed beads
- 2 small soldered jump rings
- Pair of earring findings
- Strong beading thread such as Power Pro or Fireline
- 2 #10 beading needles

Softer colors such as spring green and silver work for year-round wear.

TIP "Up" and "down" in these instructions refer to the direction of the work when the piece is turned in its wearable direction; that is, up is toward the ear.

STEP 1 Fold 1 yd. (.9 m) of thread in half, and attach the loop with a lark's head knot to a jump ring. Thread a needle on each end.

STEP 2 First side
With one thread, pick up two 11º seed beads and seven 1.5 mm cube beads. Go through the fourth and third cubes from the needle again to form a box of four beads. Pick up an 11º, and go back up four of the beads above it. Pick up a 3 mm, and go down through the two return beads.

STEP 3 Pick up five 1.5 mms. Go back through the fourth and third beads again as before. Pick up an 11º, and go back through the four beads above it. * Pick up two 3 mms. Go through the first 3 mm again in the same direction

and down through the two return beads [a]. Adjust the two 3 mms so they lie next to each other.

STEP 4 Repeat Step 3 to finish the first side [b].

STEP 5 Second side
With the remaining thread, repeat Step 2, but use the 3 mm already in the work instead of adding a new one.

STEP 6 Repeat Step 3, but use the second 3 mm you added on the first side [c].

STEP 7 Repeat Step 3 again to the *. Pick up a 3 mm and go up through the 3 mm on the opposite side, back down the 3 mm just picked up, and down through the two return beads just made [d]. Adjust the row of three 3 mm cubes to fit side by side,

and tighten the slack. This finishes the second side.

STEP 8 Bottom
With either thread, pick up an 11º, and go back up the two return beads. Pick up two 1.5 mms, and go up the previous set of return beads [e], then back down the two beads just picked up. This fastens the four beads together.

STEP 9 Repeat Step 8.

STEP 10 Pick up an 11º, and go back up only one of the cubes above it [f]. Pick up a 1.5 mm, and go up through the adjacent pair of 1.5 mms and the 3 mm in the center above [g]. You have attached the new cube to the adjacent cube in the previous row.

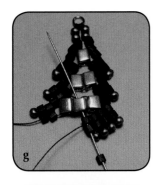

Another lovely evergreen color palette.

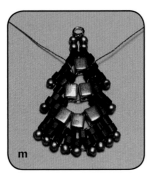

STEP 11 With the other thread, repeat Steps 8 and 9.

STEP 12 Pick up an 11º, go back up one of the two return beads, down through the single 1.5 mm you added on the other side, back up the original 1.5 mm, and down the same 1.5 mm on the other side. Pick up an 11º, and go up through the two 1.5 mms on the side just worked, and up through the center 3 mm **[h]**. Both threads will be coming out the center 3 mm. This finishes the bottom.

STEP 13 Pulling together
This final pass pulls the whole piece together. Take one thread down through the adjacent 3 mm to the outside, move farther to the outside, and go up through the three upper cubes of the lowest five-cube branch and the center 3 mm **[i]**, then go up the 1.5 mm and 3 mm of the next-higher branch **[j]**. Go through the 1.5 mm above the highest 3 mm **[k]**. Cross to the other side and go down four cubes **[l]** and up the adjacent 1.5 mm just below the 3 mm. Repeat with the other thread. The threads will now be crossed under the group of four 11ºs, and the threads should be

coming up and out just below the single upper 3 mm from opposite sides **[m]**.

STEP 14 Tie the two threads together with a surgeon's knot. Pull both ends up into the 3 mm just above the knot. Run each thread out into the work, and trim.

STEP 15 Attach an earring finding.

STEP 16 Make a second earring to match the first.

Light Hearts

These hearts were originally designed in red and pink for a February charity show, and I sold out! Then I made them in other colors—green for envy, blue for sad, white for purity, purple for … well, almost any color works. I found myself drawn to wearing them for any "heart" kind of day. I bet you will, too.

To stitch the hearts, you have to work from the bottom to the top. Don't let that confuse you. Hang these hearts with a loop of ten 15º beads or use a soldered jump ring with five 15º beads on each side. Either way works fine.

a

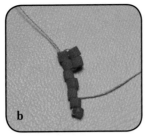

b

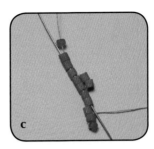

c

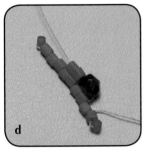

d

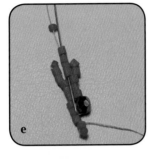

e

f

g

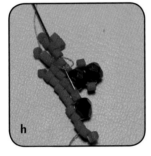

h

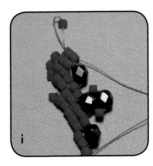

i

MATERIALS

- 2 g 1.5 mm cube beads in red
- 12 3 mm oval faceted crystals in red
- 26 15º seed beads in red
- 20 15º seed beads in silver or gold to match earring findings
- 2 3 mm soldered jump rings (optional)
- Pair of earring findings
- Beading thread
- 2 #10 or #12 beading needles

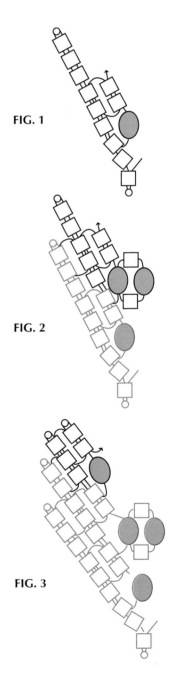

FIG. 1

FIG. 2

FIG. 3

Note: Use red 15º seed beads for the heart and silver or gold 15ºs for the loop in Step 10.

STEP 1 Thread a needle on each end of 1 yd. (.9 m) of thread. Pick up a 15º and a cube. With the other thread, go through the cube in the same direction, and center the beads [a]. This is the point of the heart.

STEP 2 First arm [fig. 1]
With one thread, pick up seven cubes, go through the fourth and third cubes from the needle again to form a box of four beads [b]. Pick up three cubes and a 15º, and go back through seven cubes [c]. Pick up an oval and go through the return beads. This is the first arm [d].

STEP 3 Second arm [fig. 2]
Pick up five cubes, and go through the fourth and third cubes again. Pick up two cubes and a 15º, and go back through four cubes [e]. Go up through the last two beads in the first arm and down through the adjacent two plus two cubes in the second arm [f].

STEP 4 Pick up an oval, a cube, an oval, and a cube. Go back through the first oval in the same direction and up through the two return beads [g].

STEP 5 Third and fourth arms [fig. 3]
Pick up five cubes, and go through the fourth and third cubes again. Pick up a 15º, and go back through three cubes, up the last two cubes in the second arm, and down the adjacent two cubes plus one more in the third arm [h]. Pick up an oval, and go through the return beads. Pick up a 15º, and go back down the two return beads [i].

TIPS
Refer to the technique sidebar on page 29 for a refresher on this stitch.

• Take out slack as you go, but don't work so tightly that you can't get a needle between two adjacent cubes.

• When you pick up a group of cubes plus a 15º, push the cubes against the work to see how many cubes you are going back through.

• For this design, rotate the return beads toward the center of the work.

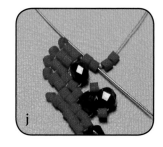
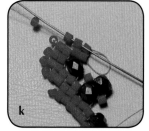
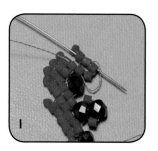

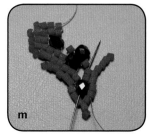
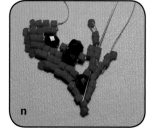
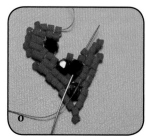

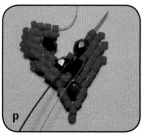
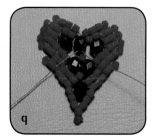
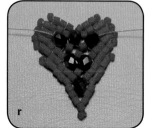

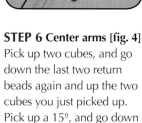
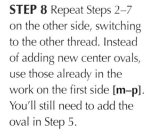

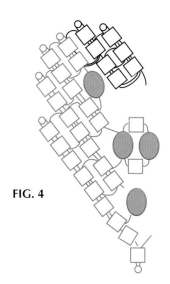

FIG. 4

STEP 6 Center arms [fig. 4] Pick up two cubes, and go down the last two return beads again and up the two cubes you just picked up. Pick up a 15º, and go down the two cubes below it.

STEP 7 Pick up four cubes, and go through the fourth and third beads again **[j]**. Turn the cubes so the first two beads you picked up are adjacent to the last oval. Go up through the return beads. Pick up a cube and a 15º, go back through the two cubes below **[k]**, up through the two adjacent cubes in the previous arm, and back down the adjacent three cubes **[l]**.

STEP 8 Repeat Steps 2–7 on the other side, switching to the other thread. Instead of adding new center ovals, use those already in the work on the first side **[m–p]**. You'll still need to add the oval in Step 5.

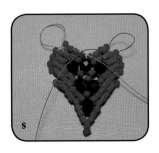

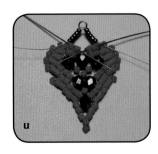

STEP 9 Closing up the center [fig. 5]
Run both threads through a new oval, pulling it down toward the center of the work **[q]**. Using each thread separately, pick up a cube, and go up the oval to the outside **[r]**, through the cube above the outer ovals, and back the other direction in the cube above it **[s]**.

STEP 10 Pick up five silver or gold 15ºs and a jump ring (or ten 15ºs), passing both threads back through the 15ºs **[t]** and down through the two cubes of the arm closest to the center of the heart **[u]**.

STEP 11 Take both threads down through the center oval again. Separate the threads, and go out through the cubes just below and to either side of the center oval and down through the two ovals on each side. Cross the threads through the cube centered below the two ovals. Go down the cubes to the right and left below, so the threads are coming out on either side and just above the top of the lowest oval. Tie off, and pull the knot into the oval. Run each thread out the first arm, and trim.

STEP 12 Attach an earring finding.

STEP 13 Make a second earring to match the first.

For Mom, Sis, or friend, heart earrings send a sweet message of affection.

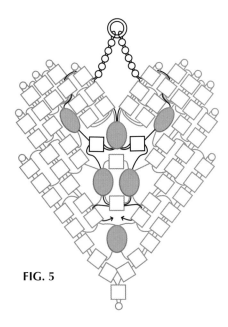

FIG. 5

Think beyond pink or red. Feeling a bit melancholy? Just want to match that blue-violet dress? Hearts can do that!

Spanish Fans

This has become one of my favorite earrings to wear. I call it Spanish Fan because my original color combination looks like a flamenco dancer's accessory. Make it in black and gold to go with more of your wardrobe. Jewel tones of teal, magenta, yellow, and orange give this same fan an Asian feel.

Be forewarned—this is probably the most challenging project in the book. Stick with it, and you'll be rewarded with an attention-getting pair of earrings.

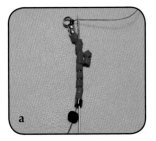

a

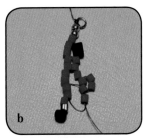

b

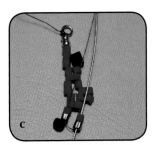

c

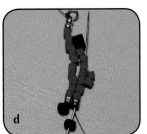

d

e

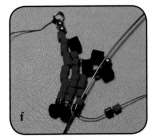

f

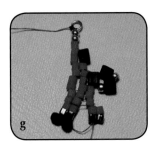

g

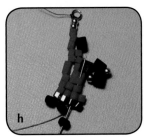

h

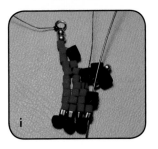

i

MATERIALS
- 28 3 mm cube beads in matte black
- 2 g 1.5 mm cube beads in matte red
- 34 1.5 mm cube beads in gold
- 34 8º seed beads in matte black
- 24 11º seed beads in gold
- 2 small soldered jump rings in gold finish
- Pair of earring findings in gold finish
- Beading thread
- #10 beading needle

Note: All 1.5 mm beads are referred to by their color, either gold or red. "Up" and "down" refer to the direction when the earring is on the ear.

STEP 1 Fold 1½ yd. (1.4 m) of thread in half, and attach the loop to a jump ring with a lark's head knot. Thread a needle on each end. Add two half hitches on either side to spread the threads farther apart around the ring.

STEP 2
Base and first arm [fig. 1]
With one needle, pick up two 11º seed beads and seven red cube beads. Go through the fourth and third beads from the needle again to form a box of four beads. Pick up five red cubes, a gold cube, and an 8º. Go back through the ten beads

above the 8º [a]. * Pick up a 3 mm, and go down through the two return beads.

STEP 3 Second arm [fig. 2]
Pick up five red cubes, and go through the fourth and third cubes from the needle again. Pick up a red cube, and attach it and the red cube above it to the adjacent beads of the first arm [b]. Pick up a red cube and a gold cube, and attach them to the two adjacent cubes in the first arm [c]. Pick up an 8º, and go back through the seven cubes above it [d]. * Pick up a 3 mm, an 11º, a 3 mm, an 11º, and a 3 mm. Go back through the first 3 mm in the same direction and down through the return beads [e].

STEP 4 Third and fourth arms [fig. 3]
Pick up two red cubes, two gold cubes, and a red cube. Go through the fourth and third cubes away from the needle again [f]. Attach the fourth and third beads you just went through to the adjacent two beads in the previous arm [g]. Pick up an 8º, and go back through the four cubes above it [h]. Pick up a 3 mm, and go down through the return beads [i]. Pick up an 8º, and go back through the same return beads [j].

STEP 5 Fifth arm [fig. 4]
Pick up a red cube and a gold cube, and attach them to the adjacent red and gold cubes in the fourth arm [k]. Pick up an 8º, and go back through the red cube, the gold cube and the 3 mm [l].

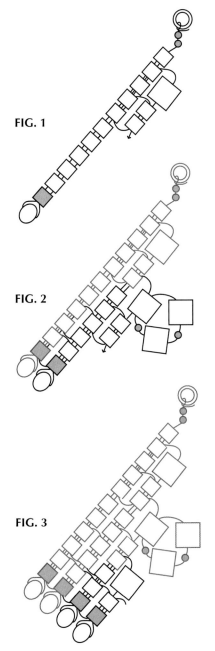

FIG. 1

FIG. 2

FIG. 3

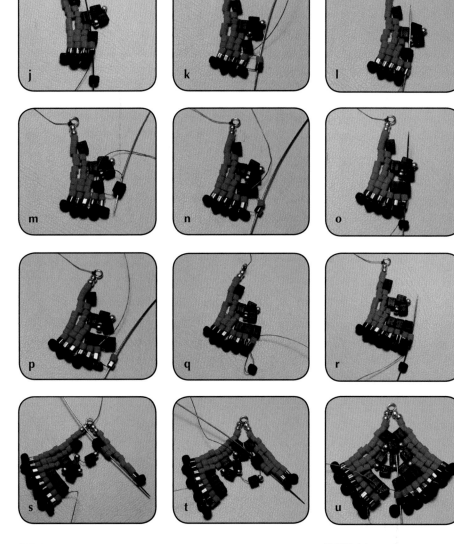

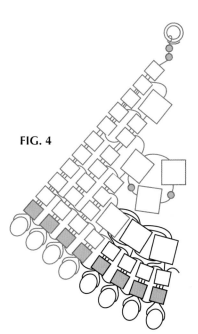

FIG. 4

STEP 6 Sixth arm [fig. 4]
Pick up a 3 mm, and attach it to the 3 mm you just came through [m]. Pick up a red cube and a gold cube, and attach them to the adjacent red and gold cubes in the sixth arm [n]. Pick up an 8º, and go back through the gold and red cubes and the 3 mm [o]. * Pick up a 3 mm, and attach it to the 3 mm you just came through.

STEP 7 Seventh arm [fig. 4]
Pick up a red cube and a gold cube, and attach them to the adjacent red and gold cubes [p]. Pick up an 8º, and

go back through the gold and red cubes above it. [q]

STEP 8 Eighth arm [fig. 4]
Repeat Step 7 [r].

OPPOSITE SIDE
STEP 9 First arm [fig. 5, blue thread]
Repeat Step 2, except at the *, pick up a 3 mm, an 11º, a 3 mm, and an 11º. Go up through the 3 mm on the first side, down through the first 3 mm you picked up in the same direction and down through the two return beads [s].

STEP 10 Second arm [fig. 5, green thread]
Repeat Step 3, except at the *, pick up a 3 mm, an 11º, and a 3 mm. Go up through the center 11º and 3 mm on the opposite side and back down the 3 mm where you started [t].

STEP 11 Remaining arms
Repeat Steps 4–8. The two sides should be identical.

STEP 12
Working up the center [fig. 5, black thread]
Add a center arm by repeating Step 7. (If the

Cube Bead Stitching   55

 v

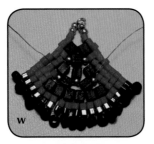 w

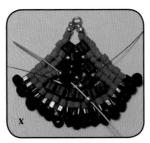 x

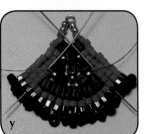 y

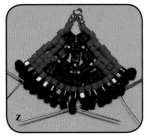 z

 aa

 bb

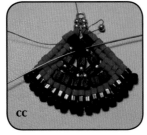 cc

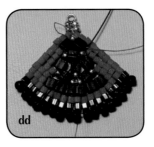 dd

A simple color change takes this design from flashy Spanish to Asian cool.

lower arms do not meet easily, add an arm to the other side as well.) Attach the red and gold cubes of the ninth arm to the red and gold cubes of the eighth arm on the other side [u]. Continue up through the 3 mm above, and attach it to the 3 mm on the other side [v]. Locate the thread coming out the first side you made, and take it up through the 3 mm above it. Attach the same two cubes again using the second thread. This secures the center firmly.

STEP 13 Now each thread is coming out one of the two center 3 mm in the bottom row of 3 mm [w]. Working separately with each thread, pick up an 11º, and go up through the 3 mm that angles off to the outside above the beads you are coming out. Go through the

11ºs [x] and the five cubes of the third arm on each side [y]. The threads will be coming out the third arm along the bottom edge.

STEP 14
Aligning the edge and finishing [fig. 5, red thread]
Working toward the far side, go through the third 8º, and run the thread through all of the 8ºs along the edge. Your threads will cross in the center. This will turn the 8ºs so the edges all face out. Adjust the tension to help the beads lie straight [z, aa].

STEP 15 Your threads are now coming out opposite ends of the row of 8ºs. Go up all the cubes in the first arm on both sides [bb]. Cross the threads and go back down the first three cubes on the opposite sides, then up the adjacent 3 mms.

Both threads are coming up out of the top two 3 mms. With one thread, pick up an 11º, and go down through the opposite 3 mm and the 11º below it [cc]. With the other thread, go through the 11º just picked up, down the opposite 3 mm and 11º [dd], and cross horizontally through the 3 mm in the center. Tie the threads together near the hole of the center cube, and pull the knot into that cube. Run the threads out the end of the second arm, and trim.

STEP 16 Attach an earring finding.

STEP 17
Make a second earring to match the first.

FIG. 5
The red line represents one thread; the other thread mirrors the first until they meet and are tied in a knot.

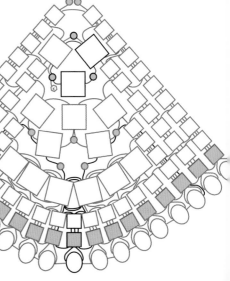

Necklaces

I didn't wear necklaces much until I started beading. Now I wear them often. I discovered that you have to pay attention to your wardrobe if you're going to wear a variety of necklaces. Certain styles of necklace work well with high necks and turtlenecks, such as the lariat or the heavier version of the Russian Waltz. I feel that the best display for a necklace is a bare neck. I own many open tops, allowing me to show off the pieces I've made. I've actually sold necklaces right off my neck!

It can be a long way around a neck when you're working a piece like the Checkered Collar or the Chain of Chevrons—anywhere from 12 to 20 in. (30–51 cm). So if you are a beginner, I suggest pacing yourself. Plan for a week or two of steady work and set short goals, like so many inches or centimeters an evening. With beading time in mind, I developed the Russian Waltz necklace in part to see if it would work to combine a stitched section for the front and a simple, quick strung section for the sides and back. That idea turned into a better design than I imagined!

Checkered Collar

Rainbow Lariat

Russian Waltz

Chain of Chevrons

I love bead collars. They frame the face in such a gentle, beautiful way and accent the neck. My interest in ancient Egypt led me to experiment with them early on, but I was disappointed that my early versions looked like part of a costume. It was a collar in *Bead&Button* magazine that started me in the right direction. I began working with two-drop peyote and found that a slight adjustment to the bottom was enough to make even a cube bead construction bend nicely around the base of the neck.

This is an elegant-looking piece of jewelry, and it's surprisingly simple to make. You may be able to follow these easy instructions even if you have little or no experience with peyote stitch. I've made these narrow collars in metallic green with light green accents, bronze-lined turquoise with silver accents, silver-lined peridot with navy accents—they all look just great.

MATERIALS
(for a 16-in./41 cm collar)
- 14 g 1.5 mm cube beads in matte ivory
- 14 g 1.5 mm cube beads in gold
- About 50 4 mm cube beads in dark gold metallic
- About 50 3 mm cube beads in dark gold metallic
- About 50 15º seed beads in dark gold
- Clasp (chain, optional)
- Beading thread
- #10 beading needle

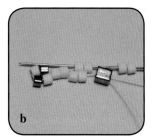

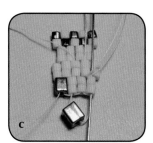

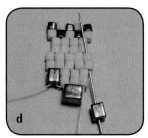

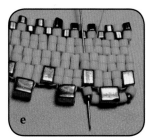

TIP I used a short length of chain for half of the clasp to make the length slightly adjustable.

Wearing collars

Collars are flattering, and not only on a long, thin neck. If they fit properly, anyone can wear one. Just be sure to make the collar long enough. The inside edge should fit just at the point where your neck starts to slope upward, but not tight enough to create a "neck muffin-top." Try to make the beadwork long enough to go all the way around the neck and meet in the back. Although I sometimes make collars with an adjustable chain extension because I don't know who is going to buy them, I prefer them with no gap at the back.

The round shape of a collar softens a pointed chin and a square jaw. Wear your bead collar under a collared shirt with just the front showing. Or wear it with a strapless top or an open neck in a V, round, square or sweetheart shape. Avoid tops that touch the collar, as they detract from its shape and effect.

STEP 1 Thread a needle with 2 yd. (1.8 m) of thread. Pick up one 3 mm, four ivory cube beads, one gold cube bead, one ivory cube, one gold cube, and one ivory cube. Go back through the fifth and sixth beads from the needle **[a]**. Pick up two ivory cubes, and go back through the 3 mm. Leaving a 12-in. (30 cm) tail, align the beads side by side, and turn so your thread is coming out the right side of the work.

STEP 2 Pick up two ivory cubes, skip over the 3 mm, and go through the next two ivory cubes **[b]**. Pick up two ivory cubes, skip two ivory cubes, and go through the ivory/gold pair. Turn.

STEP 3 Pattern
Work in the bead pattern shown **[c]**, following these simple rules: When you are working from the inside edge, always pick up an ivory/gold pair in the reverse order from the previous pair. The second pair you pick up will be ivory.

When you have added and gone back through three pairs along the outer edge, pick up a 4 mm. Go up into the third ivory pair along the bottom edge, then up through the pair in the next row up. Turn, go down the adjacent pair, and on through the pair you came out before you picked up the 4 mm bead **[c]**. You are now back where you came out the work. Pick up a 3 mm, and continue the pattern **[d]**, treating the 3 mm as you would a pair of ivory cubes. Continue this pattern until you reach the desired length, ending after a row in which you have picked up a 3 mm in order to match the ends.

Note: Keep the work pulled together tightly as you go. If you see space or thread between the beads, your tension is too loose. Pulling on the first two beads of the previous row will take up the slack. Check the tension regularly. If your work tends to be loose, take up the slack before you turn the work to do another row.

STEP 4
Finishing the lower edge
End the main part of the collar after you have picked up a 3 mm and worked back through it. Coming down out the end 3 mm, pick up an ivory cube, a 15º, and an ivory cube. * Go through the 4 mm. Pick up an ivory cube, a 15º, and an ivory cube. Go up into the next 3 mm, up and then right down through the two pair above it, down through the 3 mm, the last ivory you picked up, and the 15º **[e]**. Pick up an ivory cube, and repeat from * until you have finished the edge.

STEP 6 Sew half a clasp onto each end.

TIP You can review the basics of peyote stitch on page 26.

A fun, colorful way to use up ends or samples, this lariat can be made in any combination of rainbow colors that suits your taste or your wardrobe using either 1.5 mm or 2 mm cubes. This photo shows both versions. Drape the lariat freely around your neck, tie it in a loose knot, or double it back and put the ends through the loop like a scarf.

This is the simplest St. Petersburg chain piece in this book. It's a good place to start if you're not familiar with the stitch. You will get the feel for bringing the return beads back against the work. As you progress over the length of this piece, you'll also learn how to hold the work in your hand and develop a smooth, fast technique.

You have a lot of options for experimenting with this simple stitch. By choosing the right sequence and size of beads, you can make the chain appear to be spiraling. Or try adding intermittent diamonds or hexagons, like the geometric shapes on page 38.

MATERIALS
(for a 36-in./.9 m lariat)
- 14 g 2 mm cube beads in mixed colors
- 34 g 3 mm fringe drops in matte rainbow opaque black
- 2 g 11° seed beads to match the drops
- 2 12 mm faceted beads to match the drops
- Beading thread
- #10 beading needle

TIP A good length for a lariat is 32–42 in. (81–107 cm).

a

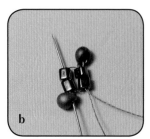
b

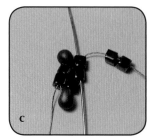
c

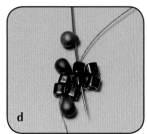
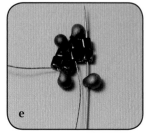
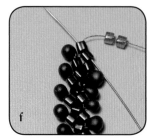

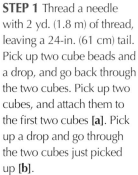
d

e

f

STEP 1 Thread a needle with 2 yd. (1.8 m) of thread, leaving a 24-in. (61 cm) tail. Pick up two cube beads and a drop, and go back through the two cubes. Pick up two cubes, and attach them to the first two cubes [a]. Pick up a drop and go through the two cubes just picked up [b].

STEP 2 Pattern
Pick up three cubes, and go through the first bead picked up and the bead you just came out again [c]. This creates two return beads. Pick up a drop, and go back through the two cubes you just came out [d]. Pick up a drop, and go through the two return beads [e].

Repeat until you reach the desired length.

To change cube colors as you stitch (from blue to green, for example), pick up one cube in the old color and two in the new color, and continue as before [f]. Change colors every 2½–3½ in. (6.4–8.9 cm).

STEP 3 At each end, pick up a 12 mm bead, and make a loop of 24 cubes alternating with 25 11ºs [g]. Go up through the 12 mm into the chain and back out to hold the loop in place [h]. Repeat twice to make two more loops. Tie off, and trim.

TIP Learn the basics of St. Petersburg chain on page 29.

Take your color cues from natural stone, as in this green, beige, and red chain that borrows from the rain forest jasper beads.

Play with the sequence of bead colors to create the look of a spiral with St. Petersburg chain. Wear the chain as is, or add a geometric pendant.

Smooth technique

Hold the work in your hand like crochet. Pick up three cubes, and slide them back to your hand. Push the three new cubes up against the previous block of four, drape them over your forefinger, and wrap the working thread around your middle finger. You are in position to pick up the last bead from the previous box and the first bead you just picked up.

Russian Waltz

As I'm working on a piece, my mind often wanders to the meaning of it. I noticed there were a number of threes in this combination of St. Petersburg chain, in particular the clusters of three silver cubes. Adding a second short stitch between the regular stitches opens up the two sides of the necklace, and they seem to hold each other apart much like dance partners. This formal dance to the count of three led me to call this necklace the Russian Waltz.

Bead weaving and gemstones combine beautifully. I think it's the contrast between the intricacy of the beadwork and the boldness of the accent beads. This design can go from delicate to dynamic just by changing the ingredients. With an elaborate necklace like this, I like to keep the earrings simple—just a single drop on an ear wire will do.

It is possible to find a couple of sizes of hollow sterling silver cubes. I've used these in combination with delicate purple crystals for a glittering look, but you can make the same design with bold glass or gemstone drops.

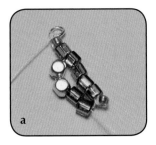

a

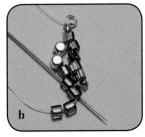

b

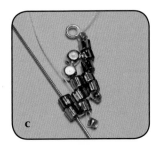

c

d

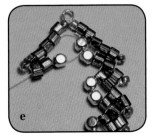

e

f

g

MATERIALS & TOOLS

- **14 g 2 mm cube beads**
- **1 g 11º seed beads to match cube beads**
- **33 4 mm sterling silver hollow cubes**
- **15 8–10 mm faceted oval beads**
- **2 small soldered jump rings**
- **2–3 ft. (61–91 cm) of 20-gauge silver wire**
- **Clasp**
- **Beading thread**
- **4 #10 beading needles**
- **Chainnose pliers**
- **Roundnose pliers**
- **Wire cutters**

Make it bold with 2 mm cubes and large pressed-glass ovals. I used flexible beading wire to complete the sides of this variation (see sidebar).

TIP Review the basics of St. Petersburg chain on page 29.

STEP 1 Fold 2¼ yd. (2.1 m) of thread in half, and attach it to a jump ring with a lark's head knot. Thread a needle on each end.

STEP 2 Inner edge
With one thread, pick up an 11º and seven 2 mm cubes. Go through the fourth and third beads from the needle again. Pick up an 11º, and go back through the four cubes above it. Pick up two silver cubes and go through the two return beads **[a]**.

STEP 3 Pick up three 2 mms. Go through the lower return bead and the first bead picked up **[b]**. Pick up an 11º, and go back through the two cubes below it and the two new return beads **[c]**.

STEP 4 Pick up four 2 mms, and go through the fourth and third cubes from the needle again. Pick up an 11º, and go back through the four cubes below it. Pick up two silver cubes, and go through the two return beads **[d]**.

STEP 5 Repeat Steps 3–4 until you have made five groups, each including two silver beads.

STEP 6 Outer edge
With the other thread, repeat Step 2, using the center silver cube to attach the two sides and picking up a silver cube before you go through the two return beads **[e]**. Repeat Steps 3–4 until you have made the second group of three silver cubes. After you go through the two return beads, pick up a 2 mm, an 11º, an oval, and an 11º. Go back through the oval, the 11º, and two cubes **[f]**.

STEP 7 Pick up two 2 mms, and attach them to the last two return beads. Pick up an 11º, and go back through the two cubes below it **[g]**. Again, pick up two 2 mms, and attach them to the last two return beads **[h]**. Pick up four 2 mms, and go through the fourth and third cubes. Pick up an 11º, and go back through the four cubes below it. Go through the center silver cube, pick up a silver cube, and go out the two return beads. You are ready to attach another oval.

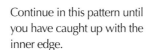

TIP You can substitute eye pins for the wire in Step 10. One end has a ready-made loop; make a loop at the other end, and trim.

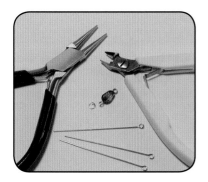

Continue in this pattern until you have caught up with the inner edge.

STEP 8 Joining the halves
Make the other half of the necklace exactly the same as the first, and lay the two halves together. On one half, continue the outer edge pattern until you have picked up the oval and come up into the work. Do the same on the other side, but instead of picking up four 2 mms, pick up only two, and use the adjacent two 2 mms on the other half to attach the two halves **[i]**. Continue up through the center silver cube, pick up

another silver cube **[j]**, and go down the four cubes on the side you are working on. Pick up an 11º, and go back up the same four cubes. You are finished with the outer edge, so work the tails to a good place, tie off, and trim.

STEP 9 With either of the two inside threads, pick up three 2 mms, and go down through the two cubes on the opposite side of the outer edge. With the other thread, go through the first cube you picked up on the first side, pick up two 2 mms, and go down the same two cubes on the other half **[k]**. Work both

tails into the work, tie off, and trim.

STEP 10 I finished my necklace with some simple wirework (see alternatives below). String an oval bead on a length of wire. Using roundnose pliers, grasp one end of the wire, and roll a small loop. Trim the opposite end of the wire to ³⁄₈ in. (1 cm), and create another loop **[l]**. Join these beaded components with jump rings, attaching an equal number to each necklace end for the desired length. Attach half of a clasp to each end.

Options for finishing the necklace sides

Here are two alternatives for completing the necklace sides (instead of creating wireworked components in Step 10). The first uses flexible beading wire and crimp beads. Cut about 12 in. (30 cm) of wire, and attach one end to the jump ring with a crimp bead. String oval and spacer beads as desired. Attach the other end of the wire to a jump ring or to half of the clasp with a crimp. Repeat to finish the other side.

For the other method, add an extra foot of thread as you begin the project. Fold the thread in half, and attach it to half of the clasp (or to a jump ring) with a lark's head knot. String oval and spacer beads on the doubled thread until you reach about a third of the desired finished length. Then simply begin the beadwork at Step 2 and end at Step 9. Make the second half the same as the first, starting from the other half of the clasp.

A chevron is a V-shaped form, repeated many times in this necklace with its mirrored St. Petersburg chain and alternating colors. The 2 mm cubes create a substantial necklace, and the drops give it added weight and accent. You'll find it works up pretty fast and looks great on the neck. You want it to hang a little lower than a collar to get the best drape.

Pick your favorite colors—the trick is finding 11° beads to match the 2 mm cubes. The large beads or drops can be round, flat, or any shape you like. If you're adventurous, try using more than two colors. You can attach a soldered jump ring in place of one or more large beads or drops, then hang all sorts of things from the rings. Try charms, clusters of pearls, or even fringe. If you prefer a bracelet, just start with a bracelet clasp—this pretty pattern looks just as good on the arm.

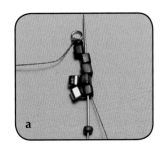
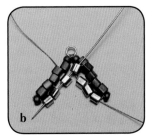

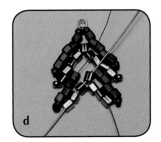
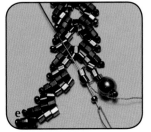

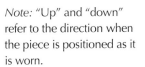

MATERIALS
(for a 15-in./38 cm necklace)
- 14 g each 2 mm cube beads in colors A and B
- About 80 each 11° seed beads in colors A and B
- 11–15 accent beads to use as drops
- 2 small soldered jump rings
- Clasp
- Beading thread
- 4 #10 beading needles

Note: "Up" and "down" refer to the direction when the piece is positioned as it is worn.

STEP 1 Fold 2¼ yd. (2.1 m) of thread in half, and attach the folded end to a jump ring using a lark's head knot. Thread a needle on each end.

STEP 2 Side
Pick up an A 11°, five A cubes, and two B cubes. Go through the fourth and third beads from the needle again. Pick up an A 11°, and go back through the four cubes above it [a]. * Pick up two B cubes, and go down through the two return beads.

STEP 3 With the other thread, repeat Step 2, but at the *, go through the upper inner B cube on the first side. Pick up another B cube, and go down through the two return beads just made [b].

STEP 4 Pick up a B cube and two A cubes, and go through the fourth and third cubes away from the needle. (The upper one will already be in the work.) [c] Pick up a B 11°, and go

back through the two cubes above it and down through the two new return beads.

STEP 5 With the other thread, repeat Step 4 on the other side.

STEP 6 Pick up two A cubes and two B cubes. Go through the fourth and third beads from the needle again. Pick up an A 11°, and go back through the four beads above it. * Pick up two B cubes, and go down through the return beads.

STEP 7 With the other thread, repeat Step 6, but at the *, go through the adjacent center cube on the first side [d]. Pick up a B cube, and go down through the return beads on the second side.

STEP 8 Repeat Steps 4–7 for about 6 in. (15 cm). After each step, take up the slack. If the work gets loose (you can see slack thread between the sides or between the beads), pull each 11° in the sequence you added it, then pull the working thread taut.

STEP 9 Center section, upper edge
To stitch the upper edge of the center section of the first half, continue work on one side only, repeating Steps 4 and 6 until you get to half the total length of the necklace.

STEP 10 Center section, lower edge
Note: In making the lower part of the center section of the first half, you will double the rows of B cubes. This helps the necklace curve nicely where it drapes down. And you will add the beads that drop down from the center section.

With the lower thread, pick up two B cubes, a drop, and a B 11°. Go back through the drop and the three cubes above it. Pick up two B cubes, and go up through the adjacent two B cubes, and back down the cubes just picked up. Pick up a B 11°, and go up the two B cubes just picked up [e]. Pick up two A cubes, go up the adjacent two B cubes, and back down the two cubes just picked up [f].

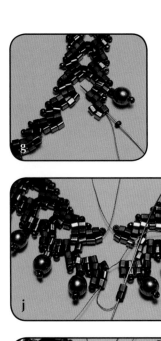

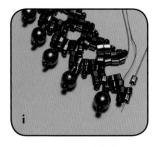

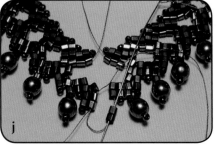

In this variation, matte black cubes and rounds are a nice foil for lustrous yellow-green cubes.

STEP 11 Pick up two A cubes and two B cubes, and go back through the fourth and third cubes from the needle. Pick up an A 11º, and go back through the four beads above it **[g]**. Go up through the top center B cube on the other side. Pick up another B cube, and go down through the two return beads on the lower edge **[h]**. Repeat Steps 10 and 11 until you have caught up with the upper side.

STEP 12 Second half
Repeat Steps 1–11 to make the second half of the necklace.

STEP 13
Joining the lower halves
Starting from either half and working on the lower edge, pick up two B cubes, a drop, and a B 11º. Go back through the drop and the three cubes above it. Attach two B cubes to the adjacent two B cubes as in Step 10. Pick up a B 11º, and go back through the two B cubes above it. Pick up two A cubes, and attach them to the adjacent B cubes, coming down out of the new A cubes. * Pick up two A cubes and two B cubes, and go through the fourth and third beads from the needle again. Pick up an A 11º, and go back through the three cubes above it. Pick up a B cube, and go down through the two B cube return beads **[i]**.

STEP 14 Using the thread coming out the other half, repeat Step 13 to the *, then pick up two A cubes and go up through the center bottom two B cubes on the first half of the necklace. Go through the two A cubes just picked up **[j]**. Pick up an A 11º, and go back through the three cubes above it **[k]**. Go down through the center three B cubes. Both threads are now coming out the same bead. With either thread, pick up two B cubes, a drop, and a B 11º. Go back through the drop and the five cubes above it. Repeat this path exactly with the other thread **[l]**. Now both threads are again coming out the same bead.

STEP 15
Joining the upper halves
With either upper thread, pick up a B 11º and a B cube. With the other upper thread, pick up a B 11º, and go through the same B cube in the opposite direction, crossing the threads and joining the two upper halves. With each thread, pick up an A 11º and an A cube, and go down the top two cubes to either side of the center row on the lower edge **[m]**. This joins the top to the bottom at the center. Tighten the work. Run the four threads out to the sides of the work so they meet, two to one side and two to the other, tie off the pairs of tails, and trim.

STEP 16 Attach each half of the clasp to a jump ring.

Beaded rings add a splash of color and a flash of charm to one's hand. These ring designs allow you to experiment with a myriad of color possibilities in a way that metal rings can't. Make something brilliant, surprising, or outrageous! If you don't want to wear them, stitch them using larger 2 mm or 3 mm cubes, and use them for napkin rings.

With tiny cubes, you can stitch a simple band that is slim enough to wear on a finger. This pattern makes a classy thumb ring. What makes this ring work is the tilelike pattern. I like it in matte-finish beads so the colors show up well.

In this project, I present a couple of peyote patterns. The first one is complete, but the second one has you try your hand at repeating the pattern.

Refer back to the Peyote Patterns bracelet for peyote stitch basics. If you're adventurous, you can also revisit the bracelet section and use 1.5 mm cubes to make finger bands out of the peyote bracelet pattern, the herringbone bracelet, and even the St. Pete bracelet.

MATERIALS

My size-8 ring uses:

- 3 g 1.5 mm cube beads in color A (red)
- 1 g 1.5 mm cube beads in color B (light blue)
- Beading thread
- #10 or #12 beading needle

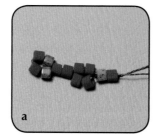

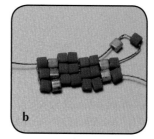

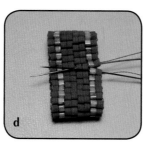

Simple Stripes

STEP 1 Thread a needle on 1½ yd. (1.4 m) of thread, and pick up an A, a B, four As, a B, and an A. Pick up an A and a B, skip the A and B last picked up, and go through the two As already on the thread in the reverse direction. Pick up two As, and go through the B and A first picked up. Straighten the beads as shown [a]. Both ends of the thread should be coming out the same bead.

STEP 2 Pattern
Pick up an A and a B, skip the next A and B, and go through two As. Pick up two As, skip two As, and go through the B and A. Turn and repeat. Just remember that you always pick up an A and B right after you turn and start a new row. The second time you pick up, it's always two As [b].

STEP 3 Continue until your ring is the desired length, ending with an even number of rows. Zip up the edges by alternating between the up beads [c]. When you get to the end of the row, both threads should be coming out adjacent beads on the edge. Thread a needle on the tail, cross the threads, and go down into the piece to pull the two sides together [d]. Tie off, and trim.

MATERIALS

My size-8 ring uses:

- 3 g 1.5 mm cube beads in color A (gold)
- 1 g 1.5 mm cube beads in color B (wine)
- Beading thread
- #10 or #12 beading needle

TIP It's important to learn to look for the pattern in your work. Each time you pick up a bead, check the spot it's going into, and see if that is the next step in your pattern. You might miss a few, but soon you'll be able to see the pattern.

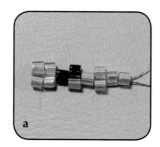

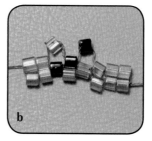

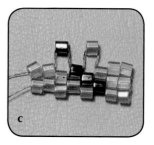

Wave Pattern

Would you like to try a pattern that is a bit more challenging? Here is a start; see if you can figure out where to place the next dark bead.

STEP 1 Pick up five As, a B, and two As. Turn. Pick up two As, skip two As, go through a B. Pick up a B, skip an A, and go through an A. Pick up an A, skip an A, and go through two As. Arrange the beads as shown [a]. Both ends of the thread should be coming out the same bead.

STEP 2 Pick up two As, skip two As, and go through an A. Pick up a B, skip an A, and go through a B. Pick up an A, skip an A, and go through two As [b]. Tighten, and turn.

STEP 3 Pick up two As, skip an A, and go through an A. Pick up an A, skip a B, and go through a B. Pick up a B, skip an A, and go through two As [c].

STEP 4 Work the pattern until your ring is the desired length. Finish as in Step 3 of the Simple Stripes band.

This is a takeoff on an expensive diamond-and-gemstone dinner ring. If you don't want to wear it yourself, it's a great addition to a child's dress-up box. I have such a box for my granddaughter, Lily, and we wear this ring when we get dressed up to visit the China Princess, one of our favorite make-believe characters.

MATERIALS

My size-7.5 ring uses:

- 2 g 1.5 mm cube beads in frosted, silver-lined
- 10 15° seed beads in frosted, silver-lined
- 3 4 mm fire-polished crystals in purple or other gemstone color
- Beading thread
- 2 #10 or #12 beading needles

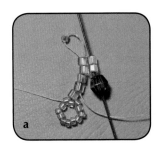 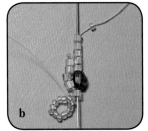 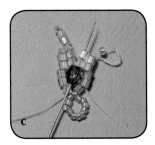

 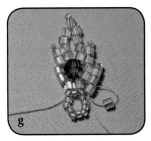 

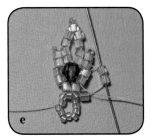  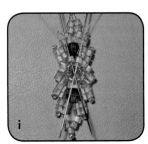

STEP 1 Thread a needle onto each end of 2 yd. (1.8 m) of thread. Pick up 12 15°s, go back through the first bead to form a ring, and center the ring on the thread. You will have two threads coming off the ring with a bead between them.

STEP 2 First long arm

With one thread, pick up seven cube beads. Go through the fourth and third cubes from the needle again. Pick up a 15°, and go back through the four cubes below it. Pick up a crystal, and go up through the two return beads [a]. * Pick up three cubes and an 11°, and go back through the three cubes you just picked up, the crystal, and the first cube on the arm [b].

STEP 3 With the other thread, repeat Step 2, but go through the existing crystal instead of adding a new one [c]. At the *, pick up two cubes, and go through the cube and the 11° at the tip of the first arm. Turn and go back down the same path as you did for the first arm to the ring [d].

STEP 4 Side arm

Bring each thread back into the ring of 15°s at the same point you exited, and go over one bead to the sides. With either thread, pick up three cubes. Attach the two cubes nearest the needle to the adjacent two cubes in the first arm [e]. Pick up an 11°, and go down to the ring [f]. Pick up a cube and attach it to the first cube in the arm [g].

STEP 5 Repeat Step 4 with the other thread.

STEP 6 Opposite long and side arms

Take both threads through the ring and around to the 15° opposite the one at the base of the first long arm. Cross the threads in that bead [h], turning the work so the new arm points upward. Repeat Steps 2–5.

STEP 7

Attaching the center oval

Take both threads back into the ring where you last exited, over, and out the two cubes at the base of the last arm made. Cross the threads, and go back down the same two cubes toward the center. This is where you will add the center oval [i].

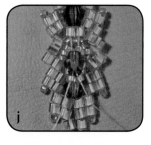

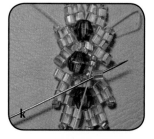

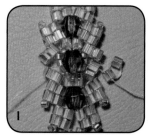

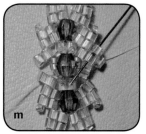

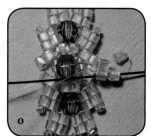

Pick up an equal number of 15ºs on both sides to center the bead over the ring [j]. This may take some trial and error. Take both threads back through the two cubes at the base of the opposite long arm.

STEP 8 Starting the band
Take one thread out the two cubes your needle is headed toward, turn toward the ring, and go through the adjacent three-cube arm, into the ring, over through two 15ºs, and out the single bead arm on the opposite side [k]. You are in position to start the band. Pick up two cubes, and go through the first cube picked up again [l]. Go back through the second cube picked up and the single cube at the base of the other side arm [m]. Go through the center side bead in the ring and back out the two beads where you started

this step [n]. These two cubes are the beginning of the band.

STEP 9 The band pattern
Pick up two cubes. Go back into the upper of the two original cubes. Turn, and go through the lower cube and the first new bead just added [o]. ** Pick up two cubes. Go back into two cubes in the opposite side, through two cubes on the original side, and through the first bead just picked up [p]. This creates an overlap and strengthens the band. Continue repeating from the ** until you are about halfway around the band.

STEP 10 With the other thread, repeat Steps 8–9, working the band from the other side until the band is the desired total length. Join the ends by stitching in a circle back and forth through each side. Make the fit snug because the tension will loosen a bit. Tie off, and trim.

74

Medallion

This ring uses the same technique as the Sunburst Medallion bracelet and most of the decorative pendants in the next chapter—a ring of tiny seed beads establishes the center, arms are attached around the ring, and the arms are fastened to each other. If you have a flat bead that you want to show off, this is a good setting for it.

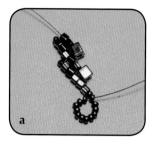

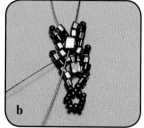

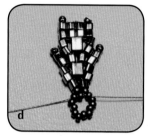

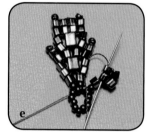

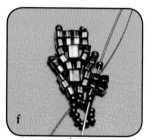

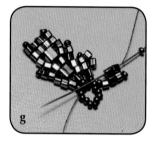

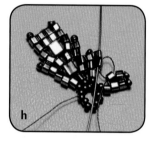

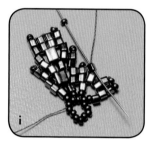

MATERIALS
- **4 3 mm cube beads in gold**
- **3 g 1.5 mm cube beads in gold**
- **1 g 15º seed beads in gold**
- **Focal bead, 12 mm across hole line, preferably flat**
- **Beading thread**
- **2 #10 beading needles**

TIP The arms incorporate St. Petersburg double chain. For a refresher on the basics of the stitch, see page 29.

STEP 1 Thread a needle on each end of 2 yd. (1.8 m) of thread. Pick up 12 11ºs, go back through the first bead to form a ring, and center the ring on the thread. You will have two threads coming off the ring with a bead between them.

STEP 2 First long arm
With one thread, pick up a 15º and seven 1.5 mm cubes. Go through the fourth and third beads from the needle again. Pick up a 15º, and go back through the four beads below it. Pick up a 3 mm cube, then go out the two return beads.

STEP 3 Pick up five 1.5 mms, and go through the fourth and third cubes from the needle again. Pick up a 15º, and go back through the four beads below it. Pick up a 3 mm,

and go through the two return beads [a].

STEP 4 Second long arm
Repeat Steps 2–3 with the other thread, but use the same center 3 mms already in the work [b]. Bring each thread back to the ring of 11ºs by crossing the two threads and coming down the opposite arms, through two 1.5 mms, the 3 mm, over and down the next 1.5 mm and 3 mm, and over and down the beginning 1.5 mm and 15º [c]. Take both threads into the original ring and over one bead, so you are coming out the spaces to the sides of the starting spaces [d].

STEP 5 First side arm
Pick up a 15º and five 1.5 mms. Go through the fourth and third beads from

the needle again, and rotate the return beads away from the long arm. Attach the top two 1.5 mms (not the return beads) to the adjacent two 1.5 mms in the long arm [e]. Pick up a 15º, go back through the two 1.5 mms and the 15º below it [f], then on through the 15º next over in the ring.

STEP 6 Second side arm
Pick up a 15º and five 1.5 mms, go through the fourth and third beads again, and rotate the return beads toward the arm just made. * Pick up a 15º, and go back through the two 1.5 mms below it. Go up through the two return beads. Pick up a 15º, and go back through the two return beads [g]. Attach the bottom new return bead (your thread is coming out of it) to the bottom return

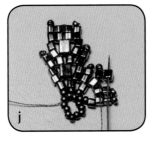

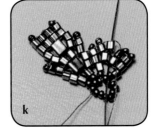

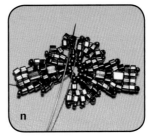

bead in the last arm made. Go out the second return bead [h]. Pick up a 15º, and go back through the 1.5 mm below it [i].

STEP 7 Now we are going to add a short half-arm to fill the gap between the first and second side arms. This is the trickiest part, so go slow and be patient.

Pick up a 1.5 mm, and attach it to the 1.5 mm you just came out [j]. Attach the new 1.5 mm to the 1.5 mm in the adjacent side arm [k]. (You may have to help this bead fit evenly between the other two. Push the beads into place, and tug gently a couple of times on the thread to take out the slack.) Pick up a 15º, and go back through the 1.5 mm you added and the 1.5 mm below it on the arm just made. Continue through the next-lowest 1.5 mm and

the 15º of the second side arm [l]. You are back at the center ring.

STEP 8 Using the other thread, repeat Steps 5–7 to make the side arms on the other side. When you are done, you will have finished half of the center medallion.

STEP 9 Opposite side of the medallion
Run the threads into the center ring and over four beads, so they cross in the bead opposite the first starting bead. Rotate the piece so you are working at the top [m]. Repeat the entire first half of the center section, Steps 2–8, except at the * of Step 6, attach the two 1.5 mms you are coming out to the adjacent two 1.5 mms of the arm of the first side [n]. Then continue to repeat Steps 6–8.

Note: The medallion may be a bit warped here as if there are too many beads, but this will adjust itself when you add the focal bead.

Once you have finished these steps, you should have worked all the way around the medallion and attached all the arms to each other.

STEP 10 Adding the focal bead
Work the two threads back through the ring, out the 15º and 1.5 mms on each long side, and through the center 3 mm. Then, take each thread through its respective 1.5 mm, turn, and go down the three 1.5 mms on the sides of the 3 mm cube [o]. Pass the threads through the focal bead using 15ºs on each side of the bead to center it.

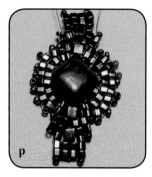

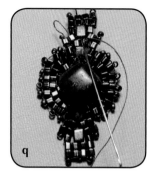

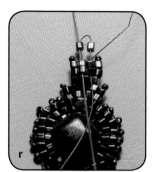

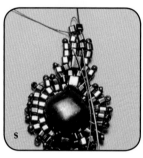

Leaving the focal bead and its adjusting beads, go through the same beads you came out on the opposite side of the medallion, then continue all the way through the long arms of the piece [p]. Turn, and go down the two adjacent 1.5 mms. Turn again, and go up the 3 mm and out the two center 1.5 mms at the end of the opposite long arm [q]. From this point, you will make the band.

STEP 11 Band
With either thread, pick up two 1.5 mms. Go back into the two cubes on the other side of the band, turn, and go through the original side of the band and the first new bead just added [r].

* With the other thread, go through the first of the two cubes just picked up, pick up two 1.5 mms; go back into two 1.5 mms in the opposite side, and out two 1.5 mms on the original side and the first bead just picked up [s]. This reinforces the stitch and strengthens the band.

Continue repeating from the * until you reach the desired length. Make a few passes to attach the band securely. Make your fit snug, because the band tension will loosen a bit. Tie off, and trim.

The gold setting of the medallion highlights the gold flecks in the lapis lazuli gemstone bead.

Decorative Pendants

These decorative pendants have so many lovely uses. I can envision an entire Christmas tree covered with beautiful, glittering snowflakes. I can imagine a window adorned with stars or flowers. But they can decorate more than just your home. Turn any one of these into a beautiful necklace or a pair of earrings. If you're a crafter, attach a star to a decorated box, or sew a cross on your jacket. Have fun with these!

All of the pendant projects play off the principles of St. Petersburg chain. If you've made the bracelet or ring design that features a focal stone, you'll recognize my technique of adding a series of St. Pete arms around a ring of beads. I've enjoyed exploring a number of variations, but the one that works best starts with small seed beads, 11ºs or 15ºs, in a ring of 12. And if you don't add the first small seed bead at the very beginning of each arm, the beads get crowded and don't fit.

Be patient with these. It may seem I'm asking you to take your thread on impossible paths at times—and there may be more than one way to put these together. But you can trust that I've done every one of them many times, and if I had found an easier way, I surely would have opted for it. Once you've made just one, making another will be a lot easier.

Maltese Cross

Winged Star

Snowflakes

Star of the East

This eight-armed cross has its origins in the Crusades. It was known as the symbol of the Christian warrior, its eight points representing the noble aspirations of the knights who bore it. When the Knights of St. John of Jerusalem took possession of the islands of Malta in 1530, the cross entered the culture and heritage of this Mediterranean archipelago, adorning everything from architecture to currency.

This design is probably the easiest of the decorative pieces. It begins not with a ring of beads but with a box. These instructions highlight the center cross in silver with contrasting color on the arms; slight variations can produce a Celtic version or even a four-sided Iron Cross. Hang yours on a chain, decorate a box, or tack it to a jacket.

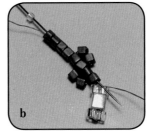

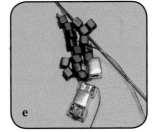

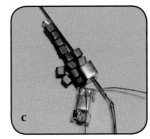

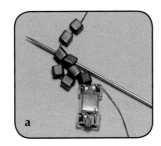

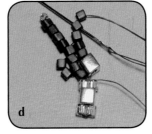

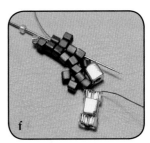

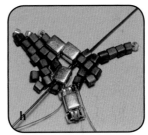

MATERIALS

- 17 3 mm cube beads in silver
- 14 g 1.5 mm cube beads in dark gray
- 8 1.5 mm cube beads in silver or silver-lined
- 30 15º seed beads in silver
- Beading thread
- 2 #10 beading needles
- Soldered jump ring (optional)

TIP If you want to attach a jump ring to hang this pendant, a good place to do it is at the end of the first arm. Attach it to the two 3 mm cubes that are angled outward. Use a bridge of three 15º beads on each side to center the jump ring.

STEP 1 Center box
Thread a needle on each end of 2 yd. (1.8 m) of thread. Using one thread, pick up a silver 1.5 mm cube, a 3 mm, and two silver 1.5 mms. Go back through the 3 mm, and pick up another silver 1.5 mm. Center these on the thread. Cross the threads, and take each thread through the 1.5 mms, the 3 mm, and the 1.5 mms to form the center.

Note: Use dark gray cubes when 1.5 mms are referenced in the following steps, unless otherwise stated.

STEP 2 Upper arm of the cross, first side
Starting with the thread on the left, pick up five 1.5 mms. Go through the fourth and third cubes from

the needle again to form a box of four beads with two return beads. Rotate the return beads toward the outside of the arm.

STEP 3 Pick up three 1.5 mms, and go through the last bead in the arm and the third cube away from the needle again, as before [a]. Rotate these return beads toward the center of the arm. Pick up four 1.5 mms and a 15º, and go back through the eight cubes below the 15º [b]. Pick up a 3 mm, and go up the last set of return beads [c].

STEP 4 Pick up three 1.5 mms and go through the second cube from the needle again, creating a return bead. Rotate the return bead toward the center of the arm [d]. Pick up a 1.5 mm, and

go down through the two adjacent 1.5 mms in the first arm and back up the two adjacent beads in the arm just made [e]. This attaches the second arm securely to the first arm. Pick up a 15º, and go back down the four cubes below it [f]. Pick up a 3 mm, and go up the single return bead. Pick up a 15º, and go down through the 1.5 mm and the 3 mm below it. Pick up another 3 mm, and go down through the 3 mm below that [g]. You are back at the center box.

STEP 5 Upper arm of the cross, second side
The second side is a mirror image of the first, except that you go through the same three 3 mms in the same order [h].

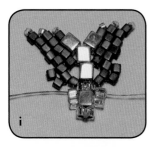 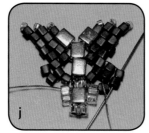 

When you have finished the second side, both threads should be coming out the two starting 1.5 mm silver cubes. * With each thread, pick up two silver 1.5 mms, and go back through the first cube you picked up. Pull these up against the work and turn them as shown in the photo [i].

STEP 6 Left and right arms
Pick up three 1.5 mms, and attach the two cubes nearest the needle to the return beads of the first arm [j]. Repeat Steps 3–4 until you are back at the center box. When you have finished both sides, bring each thread back through the starting silver 1.5 mm, the 3 mm on the side opposite the first point, and out the respective silver 1.5 mm [k].

STEP 7
Lower arm of the cross
Turn the piece upside down, and repeat the entire upper arm, Steps 2–5 to the *. Take each thread out the remaining silver 1.5 mm.

STEP 8 Left and right arms, second side
Repeat Step 6 on both sides, remembering to attach the arms at the return beads [l]. Take each thread back through its respective silver 1.5 mm. Work the tails to a place where you can tie them off, and trim.

Emphasize the circle with gold cubes to suggest a Celtic cross.

Winged Star

Whether made up in gold or silver, this star shines radiantly. I love the texture of the frosted, silver-lined cubes, and the design enhances the way the light reflects off the surface. This would be a great gift to hang from the car mirror, in a window, or on a chain. Make at least two—one for yourself and one to give away.

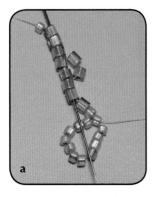

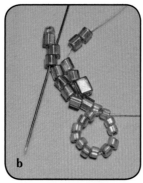

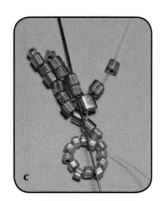

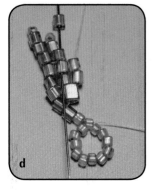

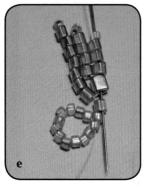

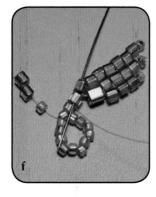

MATERIALS
• 6 3 mm cube beads in gold metallic or silver-lined gold frosted
• 14 g 2 mm cube beads in silver-lined gold frosted
• 14 g 11º beads in silver-lined gold frosted
• Soldered jump ring (optional)
• Beading thread
• #10 beading needle

This star is made one point at a time, progressing around a ring of 11º beads. Each point has four arms. Ranging from shortest to longest, the arms are made third, second, and first, then you back up to make the fourth, attaching it to the third arm as you go. In Part 1 of each point, you will make the three shorter arms. In Part 2, you will make the longest arm.

STEP 1 Thread a needle on each end of 2¼ yd. (2.1 m) of thread. Using one needle, pick up 12 11º beads. Go through the first 11º again to make a ring, and center the ring on the thread.

Note: Don't pull the ring too tight or let it be too loose. Keep your work taut, but not so jammed together that you can't get your needle between the beads. You can "break" the work—fold it so the beads open up—if

you're having trouble getting the needle through. Be careful not to break the edges of the beads.

STEP 2 First point, Part 1
* Pick up an 11º and seven 2 mms. Go through the fourth and third beads from the needle again to form a box of four beads with two return beads. Pick up three 2 mms and an 11º. Go back through the three 2 mms just picked up and the four 2 mms below them **[a]**. Pick up a 3 mm, and go out through the two return beads. Pick up two 2 mms, and attach them to the adjacent two 2 mms in the first arm **[b]**. Pick up an 11º, and go back through the four beads below it. Pick up two 2 mms, and attach them to the two adjacent 2 mms in the second arm **[c]**. Pick up a 2 mm, and attach it and the 2 mm below it to the adjacent two 2 mms in

the second arm **[d]**, going out the new 2 mm. Pick up an 11º, and go back through the three 2 mms, the 3 mm, ** and the first 2 mm **[e]**. Go through the 11º picked up at the start of this step. Your thread is now back at the ring.

STEP 3 First point, Part 2
Using the other thread, pick up an 11º and two 2 mms. Attach the two 2 mms to the adjacent two 2 mms in the first arm you made **[f]**, coming up out the two new 2 mms. Pick up four 2 mms, and attach the third and fourth beads you picked up to the fourth and fifth 2 mms in the first arm **[g]**. Pick up two 2 mms, and attach them to the two adjacent beads in the first arm **[h]**. Pick up a 2 mm, and attach it and the 2 mm below it to the adjacent beads in the first arm **[i]**. Pick up a 2 mm and an 11º, and go back through the 2 mm just picked up, the

Attach a larger jump ring, and string the winged star pendant on a chain.

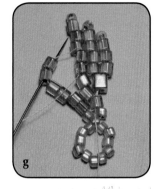

g

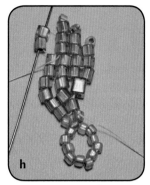

h

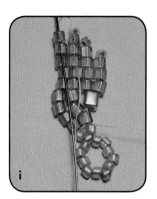

i

j

k

l

nine 2 mms below it, and the 11º at the beginning of this arm. You have finished one of the six points of the star. It should have four arms, with the longest on the left.

STEP 4
Second point, Part 1
Run each thread back into the ring and to the left through two 11ºs. Your threads should be coming out two new spaces to the left of the first point of the star **[j]**. With the thread on the right, repeat Step 2 from * to **. You will have just gone through the 3 mm; now attach the 3 mm and the 2 mm above it to the first two 2 mms in the long arm of the previous star point. Go back down the same 2 mm and 3 mm you started from and on through the first 2 mm and 11º that you started with for the second point **[k]**. You are back at the ring.

STEP 5
Second point, Part 2
Using the other thread, repeat Step 3.

STEP 6 Remaining points
Repeat Steps 4–5 for the third point. The three short arms take up more thread than the long arm, so when you come back to the ring after the third point, switch thread positions by taking the thread from the long arm through only one bead in the ring and the thread from the short arms through three beads.

STEP 8 Continue working counterclockwise, repeating Steps 4–5 until you meet the first point. When you go back down the long arm of the last point, stop before the 11º, and attach the first two 2 mms of the last arm to the adjacent 3 mm and 2 mm in the first arm you made on the first point of the star **[l]**. Go into the original ring, and take both threads over to the left to even out the tension. Sew on a jump ring, if desired, tie off, and trim.

Welcome winter with three versions of a frosty snowflake. Hang them in the window for a crystal delight, or give them as tokens at a holiday party. Tie them to a wrapped gift or tack them to a simple gift box for some sparkle. All three snowflakes can turn into a pair of earrings when made with 1.5 mm cubes. Add a faceted bead in the center for extra interest.

Shown here, starting at the left and moving counterclockwise, I give you Snowflakes 1, 2, and 3. Stitched with crystal or silver cubes, they sparkle and shine with holiday spirit, but they look just as good in pastel and pearl. If you're in a mood for spring, turn one of these into a bright blossom to reflect colorful light into a room.

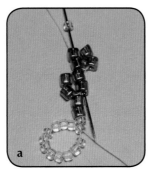

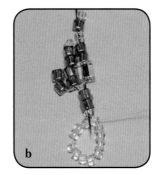

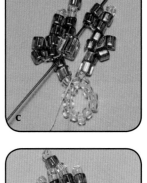

MATERIALS

(for any version of snowflake)
- **6 4 mm cube beads in white or crystal**
- **14 g 2 mm cube beads in white, crystal, or pastel**
- **1 g 11º seed beads in white or crystal (with holes large enough for at least four thread passes)**
- **Soldered jump ring (optional)**
- **Beading thread**
- **2 #10 beading needles**

TIP As in the Winged Star project, don't pull the center ring too tight or let it be too loose. You can "break" the work—fold it so the beads open up—if you're having trouble getting the needle through, but be careful not to break the bead edges.

Snowflake 1

STEP 1 Thread a needle on each end of 2 yd. (1.8 m) of thread. Using one needle, pick up 12 11º beads. Go through the first 11º again to make a ring, and center the ring on the thread.

STEP 2
First point, first side
Starting with the thread on the left, * pick up an 11º and six 2 mms. Go through the fourth and third cubes from the needle again to form a box of four beads with two return beads. Rotate these return beads toward the outside of the point.

STEP 3 Pick up four 2 mms, and go through the fourth and third cubes away from the needle again as before.

Rotate these return beads toward the center of the point. Pick up an 11º, and go back through the four cubes below it [a]. * Pick up a 4 mm, and go up the last set of return beads.

STEP 4 Pick up two 11ºs, a 2 mm, and an 11º. Go back through the 2 mm, the two 11ºs, the two 2 mms, the 4 mm, the two 2 mms, and the 11º you started with [b]. You are back at the ring.

STEP 5
First point, second side
With the thread on the right, repeat Step 2 from the *. Repeat Step 3, except at the *, don't pick up a new 4 mm, but go up through the existing one and the two 2 mms above it on the side you are working [c]. Pick up

two 11ºs, and go through the 2 mm and the 11º from the first side [d], then go all the way back down through the 2 mm, the two 11ºs, the two 2 mms, the 4 mm, the two 2 mms, and the 11º [e].

STEP 6 Bring both threads back into the circle at the space they are coming out and over through two beads to the right [f]. You are ready to make a new point to the right of the first point.

STEP 7
Second point, first side
With the thread nearest the previous point, pick up an 11º and four 2 mms. Go down through the adjacent return beads on the previous point and back up the last two 2 mms just picked up [g]. Pick up an 11º, a 2 mm,

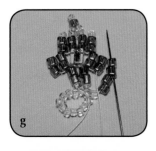

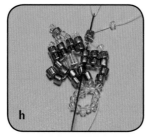

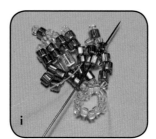

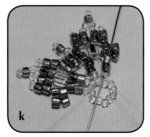

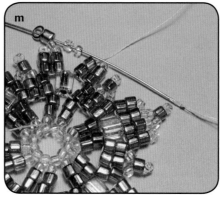

and an 11º to make a picot. Go back through the 2 mm, pick up another 11º, and go down through the two cubes adjacent to the return beads in the previous arm **[h]**. Go up through the lower return bead, then go up the last cube in the row just started **[i]**. Repeat Steps 3–4 **[j]**.

STEP 8
Second point, second side
With the other thread, repeat Step 5 **[k]**.

STEP 9 Bring both threads back into the ring at the space they are coming out and over through two beads to the right as before. You are ready to make a new point to the right of the second point.

STEP 10 Points 3–5
Repeat Steps 7–9 until you have finished five points.

STEP 11 Point 6
Repeat Step 7, but as an option, instead of adding an 11º at the tip, add a soldered jump ring and come down only through the 4 mm. Then, for the second part of the last point, pick up an 11º and four 2 mms (instead of six 2 mms). Go down through the first set of return beads on the first point and back up the last two 2 mms just picked up **[l]**. Continue as in Step 5, but go though the jump ring at the tip instead of the 11º **[m]**. Go all the way down the arm just made and through an 11º

of the original ring in the reverse direction. Go up to meet the previous thread coming out the 4 mm in the other half of the point. Tie off, and trim.

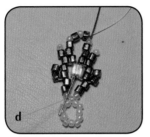

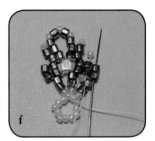

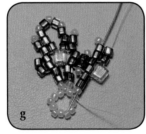

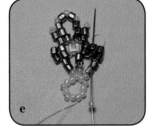

Bright color choices transform the snowflake into a spring blossom.

Snowflake 2

Follow the instructions for Snowflake 1 with these exceptions:

First point, first side

After you pick up the 4 mm and go up the return beads in Step 2, go immediately back down the first arm to the ring [a].

First point, second side

After you go through the 4 mm and the return beads on the second side in Step 5, make a different tip. Pick up a 2 mm, an 11º, a 2 mm, an 11º, a 2 mm, an 11º, and a 2 mm, and go down the two return beads on the first side [b]. Go up and over at an angle to the upper return

bead [c], back through the sequence you just picked up [d], then down the arm you just made to the ring.

Second and subsequent points

After you join the second point to the first in Step 7, instead of making a picot, go down the return beads, and pick up an 11º [e]. Turn, go up the return beads, and pick up another 11º. Go back down the return beads, then back up the last two 2 mms in the arm just made [f]. Continue as in the first point, first side [g]. For the second side, repeat as in the first point, second side.

Finish as in Snowflake 1 by closing the gap and tying off. If you want to attach a jump ring, do it on the last arm. Pick up a 2 mm, an 11º, and a 2 mm. Go through the jump ring and back down the five beads below it. Cross to the other side of the point, and go out the two 2 mm. Pick up a 2 mm, an 11º, and a 2 mm. Go through the jump ring and back through the sequence below to a point where you can tie off [h]. Trim.

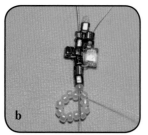

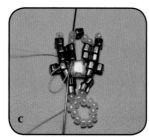

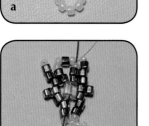

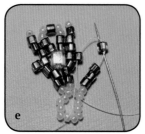

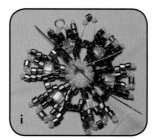

Made in gray and gold and spotlighting a gemstone bead, the snowflake is transformed into a medallion.

Snowflake 3

Follow the instructions for Snowflake 1 with these exceptions:

Start with 2¼ yd. (2.1 m) of thread.

First point, first side

In Step 1, pick up an 11º and five 2 mms. Go through the second bead away from the needle again, making only one return bead. Pick up four 2 mms, and go through the fourth and third beads from the needle again [a]. Pick up a 2 mm and an 11º, then go down the cube just picked up and the four cubes below it. Turn and pick up the 4 mm, and go up the two return beads and back down the arm to the ring [b].

First point, second side

In Step 5, pick up an 11º and five 2 mms, and make one return bead as before. Proceed as in the first half. When you come to the tip, pick up two 11ºs, a 2 mm, and two 11ºs, and go down the two return beads on the first half. Go over and up one bead, over at an angle to the upper return bead, and back through the sequence just picked up [c]. Go down the second arm though the 4 mm [d], and on to the ring.

Second point, first side

In Step 7, pick up an 11º and four 2 mms. Go down into the single return bead on the second half of the first point and back up the last bead just picked up [e]. Don't make a picot; continue as in the first point [f].

Subsequent points

Continue as in Steps 10–11 of Snowflake 1, remembering to attach a jump ring to one of the arms.

Attach the last point to the first [g]. Pick up two 11ºs and a jump ring, and go back through the two 11ºs and out the adjacent two 2 mms. Pick up two 11ºs, go through the jump ring again and back down to the original ring [h].

Finishing

Attach additional elements after you finish the main form. Follow any convenient path around the middle of the snowflake, adding an 11º, a 2 mm, and an 11º between each arm [i]. Work the threads to a convenient point, tie off, and trim.

Stitched with 1.5 mm and 3 mm cubes, any of the snowflakes can become earrings or a petite pendant.

Star of the East

This is the star I remember from childhood pictures of the nativity, guiding the Magi to the manger and the baby Jesus. There is also a remarkable connection with the planet Venus, known also as the evening star. In ancient times, Venus was already connected to the birth of a king.

Hang this on the tree, decorate a box, sew it on a jacket, or attach a pin back and wear it as a brooch.

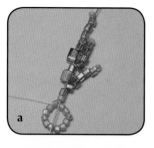

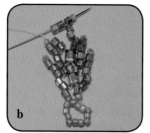

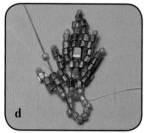

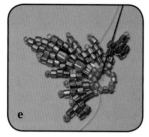

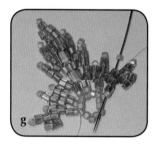

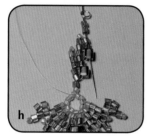

MATERIALS
- 4 4 mm cube beads
- 14 g 2 mm cubes in silver-lined frosted
- 25 11º seed beads in silver
- 4–6 mm clear faceted crystal
- Soldered jump ring (optional)
- Beading thread
- 2 #10 beading needles

Note: You'll begin at the bottom half of this piece, stitch upward, turn the work 180º, work the top upward, and connect the sides.

STEP 1 Thread a needle on each end of 2 yd. (1.8 m) of thread. Pick up 12 11º beads, go through the first bead again to form a ring, and center the ring on the thread.

STEP 2 Bottom point
Starting with the thread on the left, pick up an 11º and seven 2 mms. Go through the fourth and third beads away from the needle again to form a box with two return beads. Rotate these toward the center of the point. Pick up a 2 mm and an 11º. Go back through the 2 mm just picked up and the four 2 mms below it. Pick up a 4 mm, and go through the return beads.

STEP 3 Pick up five 2 mms. Go through the fourth and third beads away from the needle again as before. Pick up an 11º, and go down through the four 2 mms below it. Pick up a 4 mm, and go up through the return beads. * Pick up three 2 mms and an 11º. Go down through the three 2 mms just picked up, the two 2 mms below, the 4 mm, the 2 mm, the 4 mm, the 2 mm, and the 11º, which brings you back to the original ring [a].

STEP 4 With the other thread, repeat Steps 2–3, using the 4 mms already in the work. At the * in Step 3, pick up two 2 mms, and go out through the 2 mm and 11º at the tip of the point [b]. Turn, and come back through the same path along

the new arm to the center ring.

STEP 5 Take each thread into the original ring at the point you came out and over through one bead to the sides.

STEP 6 Bottom sides
Pick up an 11º and five 2 mms. Go through the fourth and third beads again as before. Go back down the two return beads, and attach them to the adjacent two 2 mms in the first arm [c]. Go through the second and third 2 mm in the arm just made. Pick up a 2 mm and an 11º, and go back through the 2 mm just picked up and the two 2 mms below it. Go back through the return beads, pick up an 11º, and go back down the same

This star glistens with iridescent blues and purples.

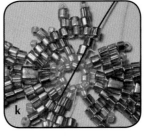

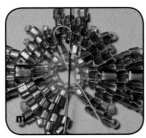

return beads. Go through the 2 mm and 11º at the beginning of this arm **[d]**. You are back at the ring.

STEP 7 Repeat Step 6 with the other thread. Take each thread back into the ring and over one bead to the side.

STEP 8 With one thread, pick up an 11º and four 2 mms. Go through the second bead away from the needle again to form a return bead, and rotate it toward the first point. ** Pick up three 2 mms, and go through the third bead in the arm just made and the first bead just picked up again, creating two return beads. Rotate these away from the first point. Pick up a 2 mm and an 11º, and go back through the 2 mm just picked up and the three beads below it.

Attach the two 2 mms in the previous arm to the single return bead and the bead just below it in the arm just made **[e]**. Go up the first of the two 2 mms in the previous arm, and cross over to the single return bead **[f]**. Pick up an 11º, and go back through the single return bead, the second 2 mm, *** the first 2 mms, and the 11º in the arm just made to the ring **[g]**.

STEP 9 Using the other thread, repeat Step 8 on the other side. Take both threads into the original ring and over four beads so the threads cross in the 11º opposite the beginning 11º.

STEP 10 Top point
Turn the piece right side up, and repeat the entire first point, Steps 2–4, except when you get to the tip of the first half and are about to add the 2 mm and 11º. You can add a jump ring instead. In the second half, simply go through the jump ring and back instead of the 2 mm and 11º **[h, i]**.

STEP 11 Top sides
Repeat Steps 6 and 8 on both sides, except when you reach the ** in Step 8. Pick up only one 2 mm, and use the two return beads on the opposite sides as the return beads for the new side **[j]**. Continue with Step 8 as before **[k, l]**. At the ***, pick up a 2 mm, and attach it to the adjacent 2 mm on both sides **[m]**. Go out the bead you just picked up and the

two 2 mms above it. Again, pick up a 2 mm, and attach it to the 2 mm on both sides **[n]**, ending by coming out the center bead toward the outside. Pick up a 2 mm and an 11º, and go back through the 2 mm just picked up and the three 2 mms below it **[o]**. Continue back to the ring.

STEP 12 Finishing
Take both threads back into and around the ring so they are coming out the beads just under the original top and bottom points. Sew on the crystal bead by crossing the threads through it **[p]**. Work the threads together in the nearest arm, tie off, and trim.

My old graphic design drafting table is now my beading table. This table has supported me for many years—through cut-and-paste, drawing, designing, colored pencil work, scratchboard, bead and fiber, and now beading. This is where I am most of the time.

About my creative process

Working as a graphic designer for many years, I had ample opportunity to learn the creative process in the trenches. Clients can be demanding, and the practice of creating logos, brochures, ads, and posters gave me a lot of experience in the discipline of generating work. To keep producing even at times when you are not feeling particularly inspired or creative requires some guiding principles of design. Producing high-quality work on demand is, to me, a main difference between an amateur and a professional.

I had a good background from the start. With a natural talent for drawing, I studied art in college as my minor. After graduating, I went back to school to take courses in composition, color, and art history. Later I studied graphic design and printmaking, and took up a string of crafts including macramé, metal engraving, and repoussé. I came to beadwork years later with this foundation for design.

The most consistent trait of my creative process is growth. New designs tend to grow out of older designs. As I'm working, my thoughts are often on further possibilities: "What if I did this larger … or smaller? What if I used different beads? What if I extended this or shortened that?" Consequently, I usually have several ideas for another piece before I'm done with the one I'm on. Growth is a very solid way of working. Each piece made reinforces the technique of the last piece and adds something new to keep the feeling vital. Most of the designs in this book were created as a result of this process.

In Georgia at 8 years old, standing in front of my dad's car in my black patent-leather Mary Janes. I think you can see the same person looking out of my eyes here and years later at my work table. Do we ever truly change? Maybe we just keep rediscovering the same self in new ways.

One of the first beadwork pieces I created was this bead-and-fiber piece made for a local "Goddess" show. My tribute to Venus puts her in one of my favorite places as a child—the beach.

I've always been fascinated with the ancient Egyptians. I enjoy reading about their culture and way of viewing the world, and I try to turn the esoteric ideas into visual form. This scratchboard artwork represents Nt, an ancient goddess connected with contraction, creation, birth, and creative tension.

Finding inspiration

Look for inspiration in the world around you. For me, it's often from the plants, animals, and scenery of the Southwest, where I've lived for many years. I did a series of beaded pieces based on the Chinle Formation, an ancient bed of rock with brick-red layers. I love the graphic black and white of the Gambel's Quail that roam daily through our yard and the unique pattern on the bobcat that occasionally strolls by my window. Subtle neutrals abound in the Southwest. Just try to name them. Dove gray. Sage. Lavender. Slate. Bone. Dry, dusty colors. Mineral colors.

Color itself calls me. I need color like a tonic. Not just one color, but many. I'll feel the need to do something orange, and it won't let go of me. (Just saying the name, I can practically smell the citrus.) Then I exhaust orange and shift to red (coral reefs, persimmons, iron oxide), or the desire for contrast will come over me and I'll seek a deep, refreshing pool of blue (lapis lazuli) or green (cedar, pine, new grass, budding leaves). I'm the same way about my wardrobe. In fact, what you wear most often is a good place to discover color palette cues.

Sinbad Valley color is the result of all the beautiful layers of history within the mountains and the mineral deposits that abound in the Southwest.

You would think this photo was taken in the wilderness, but it is a view of my front yard. Just over the next ridge is the city of Grand Junction. This elegant creature sat down for a rest about 20 feet from our front window.

Challenging the masters

As a creative exercise, I'll sometimes search for a picture of beadwork that wows me. (If you live in a big city, you can see the real thing at a show of beaded work or in a high-end gallery.) I choose materials that are not duplicates of what was used in the great work, but something I like that's similar, and I try to match the level of quality—not the exact look—of the original. I want to feel proud that my work holds up side by side with the master's piece. This may seem easy, but if you have chosen elements that are slightly different, the small changes will force you to look at the master's process and learn what made the work so excellent.

Learning from the work of others is a legitimate way to increase your range and skill. It's usually part of a formal art education to copy the masters of painting. This works in beading as well—just learn from it; don't ever pass off a copy as your own or try to sell it. We're fortunate to have magazines and books in which many of the master bead artists share their techniques. Learn from them, and apply the techniques to build a body of your own beautiful, original beaded work.

Virginia Jensen

Delight in a world of creative ideas for seed beads

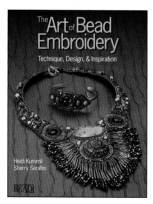